# Same Author

# Spiritual Warfare Against Witchcraft

PHILIP C SOSSOU

**author**HOUSE

*AuthorHouse™*
*1663 Liberty Drive*
*Bloomington, IN 47403*
*www.authorhouse.com*
*Phone: 833-262-8899*

*Published by AuthorHouse  10/03/2024*

*ISBN: 979-8-8230-3533-0 (sc)*
*ISBN: 979-8-8230-3532-3 (e)*

*Library of Congress Control Number: 2024921224*

# Contents

# Contents

## Part 1

## Part 2

# Book Dedication

This book is dedicated primarily to my family members. My wife and two kids were around me during my years of battle against witches and wizards. The enemy tried to use them against me and me against them. But, with our devotion to the call of the Almighty on our family, we had victory at every step of the way. At times, we didn't have food to eat, but we didn't give up. We knew as long as Jesus was in our boat, we would make it through the raging storms. The challenges were enormous, but we pulled it through with His hands on us. All my recognition to the Almighty, who had confidence in me to assign this task to my humble personality.

# Spiritual Warfare Against Witchcraft

Our God is good. Every child that's born of a woman is perfectly protected spiritually. A spiritual hedge surrounds the child at birth. It's like an ancient city surrounded by a ticking wall. A child customarily born and left in a room full of demons remains untouched and secured. Every illegal infiltration is a result of legal access given to the demon. Parents can quickly provide legal access to the devil through multiple venues: doing drugs, inappropriate sex, self-cursing, self-hatred, extreme anger, and much more. In the bible, there are some key verses we need to understand to get a clear picture of the spiritual battles. In my years as a pastor and a man of God, I have seen Christians afraid of witches and wizards. Some move from one apartment to another because of a presumed witch living in the apartment complex. Some other Christians quit their jobs because a witch or wizard is at their workplace. That's why every Christian should learn the spiritual warfare against witchcraft to chase away any witches or wizards in his workplace or apartment complex.

## A. Job 1:8-10

**Then the Lord said to Satan, "Have you considered my servant Job? No one on earth likes him; he is blameless and upright, a man who fears God and avoids evil. "Does Job fear God for nothing?" Satan replied. 10 "Have you not put a hedge around him, his household, and everything he has? You have blessed the work of his hands so that his flocks and herds are spread throughout the land.**

The devil was roaming on the earth looking for who to destroy, for Jesus said the devil comes only to steal and kill and destroy. He attempted several times to steal from Job but was unsuccessful. He even attempted to kill his abilities because of the great wealth and fame he possessed. Above that, he triedto destroy Job's possessions, like houses, flocks, sheep, camels, and oxen. Even the servants who worked for Job were immune from the devil's attacks. All the endeavors of the devil didn't pay off and returned void because God erected a hedge all around Job and his possessions. To access Job, the devil had to acquire permission from God. God had to remove the hedge around Job before the enemy could touch him and his possessions. In the life of a person, whether the person is a Christian or not, there must be legal access granted to the devil before he can harm somebody. A person can open the hedge that God placed around him, giving easy access to the demonic forces to destroy his life. That is why the devil uses many devious ways to lure people into his trap. He easily seduces many people to give him access to their lives to mess them up. Satan has never done good to anybody. Instead, he torments people and keeps them close to himself to finally lead them to hell, the final judgment. The devil's preoccupation is bringing as many people as possible to hell with him.

# B. Ecclesiastes 10:8-9

**Whoever digs a pit may fall into it;**
**whoever breaks through a wall may be bitten by a snake.**
**Whoever they may injure quarries stones;**
**whoever splits logs may be endangered by them.**

King Solomon unveils a clear picture of a spiritual truth in his wisdom. A snake will bite anyone who breaks the hedge God has around him. Meaning that anyone who removes God's protection around himself will receive a demonic visitation. If a man doesn't damage the protection God has around him, he'll be protected and safe. We can compare this situation to a sheep living in a pen alone. The pen is very secure, and no one can damage it from the outside, but only from the inside. Around the fence roam hungry wolves and bears that the sheep can't see or hear. The wolves and bears are equipped with a sweet voice to speak to the sheep's mind, making him believe that it's his mind. The wolves and bears will use their sweet voice to tell the sheep about all kinds of pleasures over the other side of the fence. Somehow, the wolves can create a burning desire in the sheep's mind to venture outside the wall. The wolves can instruct the sheep to open a hole in the fence by robbing his head on the same side of the wall. The little sheep will think that the idea of hitting the same place of the wall is coming from herself. Thus, the sheep will start robbing her head every morning on the same fence spot until a gap in the enclosure opens. Then, the wolves will come in to steal, kill, and destroy the naïve sheep.

## C. Hebrew 12:1

**Therefore, since such a great cloud of witnesses surrounds us, let us throw off everything that hinders and the sin that so easily entangles. And let us run with perseverance the race marked out for us.**

We often think we're alone in our bedroom or our closet so that we can do whatever or say whatever we want. Wrong. We're never alone. All the saints in the kingdom of God and all the evil spirits in the kingdom of the darkness watch us daily. All entities in the spiritual realm witness what we do and listen to our conversations and dialogues. They're all aware of what we do and say. Evil spirits are after the things we do and say to gather evidence against us before God to have legal access to our lives. Sometimes, just what we watch on YouTube, Facebook, and Tick Tock will grant legal access to the evil spirit that is the promotor of what we have watched. An evil spirit can be the author of a clip you watch on YouTube, Facebook, or Tick Tock. For the simple reason you have watched his clip, it allows him to request authority over your life. He'll accuse you before God, who will grant the evil spirit legal access to your life. Then, the evil spirit will start tormenting your life. Some video games are the pure work of some evil spirits. Anyone playing those video games is exposing his life to the mercy of the evil spirits, the authors of the video games.

The spiritual realm is so complex that no one can entirely pretend to understand it. We need to know a few principles about it to avoid falling into the evil spirit's traps.

# D. Matt 12:24-26

**But when the Pharisees heard this, they said, "It is only by Beelzebul, the prince of demons, that this fellow drives out demons."**

**25 Jesus knew their thoughts and said to them, "Every kingdom divided against itself will be ruined, and every city or household divided against itself will not stand. 26 If Satan drives out Satan, he is divided against himself. How, then, can his kingdom stand?**

A demon doesn't fight against another demon. There is no conflict among the evil spirits, but a vital harmony exists among them. A demon doesn't cast out another demon; instead, they negotiate. They make a transaction. They can exchange a stronger demon for a weaker demon. They do transactions and negotiations. A witch doctor can remove a deadly disease from someone's body and replace it with a less fatal disease. Only Jesus has power over them and can command them. They obey Jesus because they know who he is.

Consequently, they obey anyone with Jesus's authority on his shoulder. Sole the name of Jesus can triumph over the evil spirits. In the book of Acts, we read about the seven sons of Sevas who go around casting demons in the name of Jesus, whom Apostle Paul is preaching. One day, a demon charges some of the Sevas' sons because they don't have the authority or the calling to do so.

# E. Ephesians 6:12

**Our struggle is not against flesh and blood but against the rulers, authorities, powers of this dark world, and the spiritual forces of evil in the heavenly realms.**

The kingdom of Satan is very organized. Evil spirits constantly relay information to one another. They use deceitful means to trap people into their web. Because they watch human beings for millions of years, they know the tricks that work in every group of people. They inject their behavior into every culture on earth, especially traditions. According to some Bible scholars, the rulers of the demons reside in the second heaven around the moon and the stars we see at night. These rulers have assigned other demons with authority over every country on earth. Then, the demons with authority have numerous demons under their control that spread out in the cities and the villages of the country where they are assigned. The authority demon can move more demons to a single location according to the need. Some demons may have a lot of subjects. We see that in the case of the Asthmatic demon. The same demons can cause asthma in the lives of many asthmatic individuals. The same demon will provoke an asthmatic attack in the lungs of a victim for five minutes, then go to another victim for ten minutes and to another for five minutes. All day long, the same demon will continue in the same circle for years after years. The purpose of the demon is to steal, kill, and destroy God's creatures.

## F. Who was Satan?

His original name was Lucifer. He was a beautiful angel created by God with many different abilities. He could lead a magnificent praise and worship unto God. He had many angels under his leadership to compose songs and offer odorizing praise and sacrifices to God. In the service of his ministry to God, Lucifer became proud of himself, wishing in his heart for angels to praise him, too. Lucifer's heart desire was a sin that had no place before God. Lucifer wanted to ascend above the throne of God and make himself like God. In his elevation, Lucifer lured the angels who ministered under his leadership. So, God rejected Lucifer and the angels under his supervision. From that day, Lucifer became Satan, and his following angels turned to demons, vowing to mislead humanity away from God. God loved dearly Adam and Eve the day He made them as living souls.

**Ezekiel 28:15-17**

**From the day you were created until wickedness was found in you, you were blameless in your ways. Through your widespread trade, you were filled with violence, and you sinned. So, I drove you in disgrace from the Mount of God and expelled you, guardian cherub, from among the fiery stones. Your beauty made your heart proud, and your splendor corrupted your wisdom. So, I threw you to the earth; I made a spectacle of you before kings.**

# G. The basis of witchcraft

God made Adam and Eva with the link between their soul and spirit in the Garden of Eden. Adam and Eva can identify who comes into the garden whenever God comes into the garden. Their spirit can tell what spirit is in the Garden of Eden. Whether it's God or an evil spirit, remember that a man is composed of a body, a soul, and a spirit. In the Garden of Eden, there was a link between the body, the soul, and the spirit of Adan and Eve. They could talk to any spirit that could get close to them. When Adam was created, he was given a strict recommendation not to eat the tree's fruit of knowing right and wrong in the garden's center. God recommended Adam before Eve was made from Adam's rib. God stated clearly that he would die the day he ate the fruit. The death consisted of a cessation of contact with the spiritual realm and God. It meant that the link between the soul and the spirit of Adam would be cut off. He would no longer operate in the realm of the spirit, and his ability to deal with spiritual entities would cease. So, the day Adam and Eve transgressed the law, God removed the link between their spirit and soul. From that day, they were dead to the spirit and alive in the flesh.

Some powerful demons can temporarily establish the link between their followers' spirits and souls. When these demons develop the link between a person's soul and spirit, his soul controls his spirit. The soul of a witch in the body is aware of everything that is said and happened. That's how a person can become a witch, get out of her body, and do evil things to people. Being able to do bad things takes experience from the witch. The witch has to learn how to operate in the spiritual dimension. The witch must know all the tools at her disposal to reach her goal. The majority of the time, the witch uses an equation system. It means that if a witch puts something in your body, she also adds your reaction, triggering the consequence. But, if the victim doesn't react to the initial plan to hurt the victim, the result will not activate. For example, a witch can attach a cause of itching on your spiritual leg and pin it to your physical leg. The witch must add the object that should trigger the itches. Most of the time, a witch would choose the nails. As long as you are using your nails to scratch the itching leg, the itching will worsen. But if you use the palm of your hand or a rag to rub the itching place on your leg, it will stop.

Witches and wizards get so frustrated and furious when their plans fail repeatedly. One day, a wizard followed me to my workplace. I saw him in my car when I was driving to work. At my job, he set up a trap for me in the male restroom in a way that each time I entered the bathroom, I would feel a kind of electricity going through me. When I realized that, I went into the restroom backward and undid the trap. He was upset, and he left. Something great to do when you know you are under a witchcraft attack is to change your routine from time to time. They watch and study all your moves to find some behavior in your daily routine to set up a trap for you. If you change your routine, they need more work to find what can work. For example, change the time you go to your mailbox to get your mail. Sometimes, you can go to the trash dumpster before entering your mailbox. Or after the mailbox, go to the dumpster. Try to switch your activities and behaviors.

In my years of battle against them, I made them frustrated and angry because I understood how they operated. They got so angry when I undid every trap, they set up for me. They were just human beings, and they didn't know everything and didn't have all the power. I could undo every trap they put before so that they became furious and threatened to kill me. Sometimes, I could see them on the wall of my room, just observing all my moves to study my behaviors to know what could work. I wasn't afraid of them because I knew Jesus had overcome them over two thousand years ago.

# Part 1

Part I

# I

# What is a spiritual warfare?

A simple definition of spiritual warfare is "the Christian concept of fighting against the work of preternatural evil forces." Spiritual warfare is an ever-ending spiritual battle of a born-again Christian against evil forces. Evil spirits try daily to bring the Christians down through temptations, intimidations, and seductions. All must fight these battles to stay in flow, or they'll be backside. I need to emphasize here that it's a battle between Christians and the evil spirits roaming the world. It's not a battle between God and Satan. God and Satan are not fighting in any case. God cannot fight Satan. God has created Lucifer, who has turned into Satan. God will crush Satan if there will be a fight between these two. Satan is like an ant before an adult human being. If an adult human steps foot on an ant, he'll crush the ant to the point that no one can see a piece of the ant. God is so powerful that the devil can't stand before God to defy his order. When you read **Revelation 20:1-3**

**And I saw an angel coming out of heaven, having the key to the Abyss and holding a great chain in his hand. 2 He seized the dragon, that ancient serpent, who is the devil,**

**or Satan, and bound him for a thousand years. 3 He threw him into the Abyss and locked and sealed it over him to keep him from deceiving the nations until the thousand years were ended. After that, he must be set free for a short time.**

God gives an order to an angel to seize Satan and bind him with a heavy shackle and throw him into the Abyss. Just one angel grabs Satan, puts a shackle around him and throws him into the Abyss. Only one angel can do that to Satan, but God has trillions and trillions of angels at his service. So, if it comes to a fight between God and Satan, God will crush him in a way that there will not be a piece of Satan left on the ground. The question you'll ask is: "Why is Satan still roaming around looking for who to devour?" Quite frankly, the answer is not easy. The simple answer is that there are numerous things God cannot do, but the devil can do. God cannot lure somebody into sin. God cannot bring an accusation against a Christian. God cannot steal, kill, and destroy. The devil is very proficient in all those things. That is why God allows Satan and his allies to operate for a short period. God has set up a time when he is going to put an end to the kingdom of Satan. Beyond that, God has given Christians all the tools necessary to fight the devil and win. If the Christians can use those tools efficiently, they will defeat every force of darkness. Every Christian can potentially defeat every witch and wizard on the planet. It's sad to see that many Christians are afraid of the Witcraft. All the witches and wizards I have faced in my years of spiritual warfare testify that they realize they cannot win the battle against me. But they are going to turn against my children. I always tell them, "Jesus who defeats you will defeat you again when you approach my children." One wizard sent me a friend request on Facebook, asking to be my friend after eighteen months of brutal battle. He wanted to be my friend because he didn't know it was Jesus who had defeated him. I accepted the wizard's friend's request, hoping to convert him to Christ, but the Holy Spirit was upset with me. He told me the wizard wasn't ready to convert, so I canceled the friend request.

# II

# Behaviors that open spiritual doors

## 1. Verbal abuse or verbal curse.

When a child goes through constant verbal abuse like cursing, yelling at, harsh insults, looking down on, physically beating, or spitting on, that child will develop very low self-esteem. This child will live in isolation, rejection, and fear. The fear opens the door to any demonic spirit to have control over the child. The evil spirit will convince the child that his parents don't like him, but he (the demon) can be his best buddy. Then, the evil spirit will start using the child, teaching him what to do and where to go. This child can go from just a rebellious child to a criminal, depending on how evil the demon wants him to get. All demons have a goal. They are just waiting for a body they can have control over to perpetrate their plans.

There was a case of a child named Abdon in Africa who went through horrible abuse from his stepmother after the death of his biological mother. Abdon's mother died when he was five years old. His father got married a year later. The stepmother trashed the little boy from sunset to sundown.

One night, while crying on his bed, a feeling came to him and comforted him. The feeling was telling him not to cry anymore, for he would be his friend and tell him what to do. From that night, Abdon could sense money half a mile from him. Abdon could tell where money was hidden in school, at home, in grocery stores, and in neighboring houses. Six months after his deliverance, his father asked him: "Abdon, why you cannot steal anymore?" He explained to his father that a feeling inside was telling him where to find money. After deliverance, he couldn't sense the presence of that feeling anymore. He stated that he didn't know that feeling was an evil spirit but thought it was from his mind.

Here is where evil spirits successfully lure humankind to do things to irritate God without knowing. Some spirits arouse feelings of gratification in people who are gays and lesbians. The satisfaction they get pushes them to love the abomination lifestyle they embrace. By following their feelings, they are making themselves enemies of God. Not only that but there are also some cultures in Africa where people believe that they can get into contact with their dead ancestors. The belief of being in contact with ancestors is a pure fabrication of evil spirits to keep people's eyes away from God. Thus, people with that belief offer sacrifices to demons, thinking they are sacrificing to their ancestors. It is sad to see how evil spirits manage to lure humankind to worship them rather than worship the Creator, the Living God. He is alive well today. If you seek Him truly, He will make Himself available to you.

## 2. Minor sexual activities.

Minors who are engaged voluntarily in sexual activities open doors to evil spirits who can infiltrate their lives. Most of the underage sex is an invitation to a sexual spirit. A girl who is not yet 15 years old and who deliberately, knowingly, and willingly has sex exposes herself to a sexual demon. The demon will make a hold on her to increase the desire to have sex in her. So, the young girl will crave sex all the time and look for occasions to have sex. The sexual demon isn't invited, but he invites himself into the scene. Remember this Bible verse, **Hebrew 12:1**. We do nothing in the closet. There is a great multitude of witnesses that watch us every day. Physical eyes may not see you in your closet, but there are a lot of spiritual eyes on you in your daily activities. Nothing is hidden before those eyes in the spiritual realm. According to spiritual world, "what happens in Vegas doesn't stay in Vegas." Every entity in the spiritual realm is aware of the occurrences. Surely, consequences will follow your destructive behaviors. The evil spirit will cause young girls to crave sexual intercourse to hurt a lot of guys or themselves in the process. The evil spirit's purpose is to destroy someone's life or steal someone's bright future. For that reason, the young girl will abandon early school or will lose interest in school. She may become pregnant or contract a deadly disease.

## 3. Adults forced to have sex or rape.

Rape is a sexual violence no one should inflict on a woman because of the devastating effects that follow. After a rape, many evil spirits take control over the mind of the victim through self-blame and guilt. The way the victim always gets decimated makes me think there are many demons involved with the rape victims.

The first thing the victims realize is that the event seems never to leave them. They always remember the act of the rape, the feeling they have gone through, the environment of the act, the perpetrator, and much more. The devil uses the flashback to get complete control over the victim and forces the victim to accept horrible thoughts about themselves. The evil spirits will cause the victims to fall into a deep and prolonged depression. Feeling guilty of what has happened to them, the victims blame themselves. They believe they are the cause of the rape and choose to withdraw themselves from the society. Thus, they become isolated and lose the desire to get involved in any social activities. Soon, they start to have mood swings. In one moment, they feel OK, but a short moment later, they feel rage, unrest, and retaliation. Their mood changes without an apparent reason. They also start to experience the difficulty to go to sleep. The insomnia can take over their mind, and they have to turn to smoking drugs and alcohol to make it through the night. A lot of times, during the little sleeping times they have are full of nightmares. They are even afraid to sleep because what they will see in their dreams isn't pleasant. Besides, the evil spirits will convince them not to turn to anybody for help. Most of the time, they feel that no one will believe them. So, they will hide their feeling from their parents, teachers, pastors, coaches.

# 4. You are engaging in abomination activities before God.

## a. Boys having sex with boys

Everything the word of God points out as an abomination has dire repercussions whenever somebody does it. A boy who has sex with another boy commits an abomination in the sight of God. That act only gives the right to any evil spirit to afflict the boys. Indeed, an evil spirit will get involved and grant a feeling of fulfillment to the boys and then afflict them with anxiety at the same time. The more these boys engage in these activities, the more stress and depression will overshadow their lives. A lot of school counselors report a high rate of depression and suicide among students who engage in same-sex activities. The school systems across the United States don't understand why the trend is so evident. They allocate considerable resources to combat unsuccessfully the trend. Statistics on Mental Health and Suicide among LBTQ Youth posted on Newport Academic's website compel the American Society to review the gender philosophy. The Newport Academic states that 40% of students engaged in homosexual activities consider suicide attempts. Then, 70% of these teens are subject to depression or anxiety.

## b. Girls having sex with girls

The result above applies to the girls who are engaged in same-sex activities. Whether boys or girls, if you are living in abomination, you will reap dire consequences. The situation is that God does not even consider what you are doing, but evil spirits go around looking for someone to destroy. God doesn't send them to do anything to anyone. But they know the spiritual rules and are eager to enforce them. Evil spirits don't like to be idle. They all thirst for a human body they can inhabit to do wrong. Whenever an evil spirit doesn't have a human body to use, it behaves like a little kid playing with himself. One day, the Holy Spirit opened my eyes to see an evil spirit while I was in my dining room eating with my wife and two children. I saw the spirit in my kitchen, by a microwave playing by itself. It was floating in the kitchen back and forth, aimlessly. It was not leaving the kitchen. It was just playing with itself, waiting for an occasion to get a victim. Its form was irregular, and its color was a grayish color. It was like a shadow in the mid-air. It didn't sit on the kitchen floor but was suspended in the air, going back and forth. I didn't know if the demon knew that I saw its behavior. It was the Holy Spirit who opened my eyes to see.

## 5. All cases of incest: sexual intercourse between closely related persons.

By definition, incest is intercourse between closely related persons by blood or marriage. Most of the time, it's an adult in the family who will make a move on a minor in the same family. God is very much against these kinds of behavior in any human society. In the book of Leviticus, God instructed the children of Israel against all types of incest He labeled as abominations. **Leviticus 18:6 No one is to approach any close relative to have sexual relations. I am the Lord.**

Whenever incest occurs in a family, the perpetrators fall under a curse, and any evil spirit can have access to them. The young person starts experiencing some traumatism and bipolarism. The young person will start having difficulty focusing and acting as two people in one body. Their behaviors will change according to the circumstances and the environment. Today, they will love apples; tomorrow, they will hate the same apple. Their feelings will flip-flop without a specific reason.

## 6. Doing drugs.

The use of an illegal drug like marijuana, cocaine, and methamphetamine directly affects the human brain, which will influence the user's behaviors. Every drug use changes the chemical distribution and balance in a person's brain. The first time a person uses the drugs named above, the spirit of those drugs comes into the scene to give the first-time user an incredible spiritual exaltation. The first-time user will experience a lifetime of seeing his spirit floating in the sky. The spirit of the drug will take the first-time user into the spiritual realm and offer him some sensational pleasures. The spirit of marijuana gives a different spiritual pleasure than does the spirit of cocaine, which in turn is different from the methamphetamine spirit. There is a trick behind the first enjoyable experience. The spirit behind the drug makes the first experience very exceptional. The spirit gives the first user an experience one-of-its-kind, which the drug user will long for all day of his life and will not get. The spirit of methamphetamine plays this trick very well. The methamphetamine spirit will tell the user to inject more and more of the drug to get the original experience. The more the user injects the drug, the more he will realize that the experience isn't at its top. Then, the user will repeatedly increase the dose, but the experience will never reach the ultimate climax. It is the reason why a lot of teenagers using methamphetamine die from overdose. The devil's purpose is to kill. Evil spirits don't do good to anybody. Their purpose is to harm.

## 7. Having sex with an animal.

God is very much against a person having sex with an animal. **Leviticus 20:16 If a woman approaches an animal to have sexual relations with it, kill both the woman and the animal. They are to be put to death; their blood will be on their own heads.**

Whether you are a man or a woman, you have a lifetime partner somewhere. You need God's guidance to be able to find that partner. Turning to an animal for a sexual relationship is against nature. Nature will punish you when you commit such a horrible act of having sex with an animal.

## 8. Mocking God in public or defying God.

I have seen on some talk shows where some people claim to be atheists. It's a personal business if someone claims to be an atheist or someone who believes that God doesn't exist. It's OK with God. God knows that you're ignorant. God knows that all human beings are unaware of who God is. The human brain is so limited that it cannot fancy or grasp the essence of the Creator God. The immensity of our Creator is beyond our imagination. Our brain cannot wrap around who he truly is. It's by favor that some of us can claim to know

Him. So, if you believe that God doesn't exist, I don't blame you, for it's tough to get to know Him. But don't make the mistake of mocking God in public or defying God in front of people. You'll pay that mistake with your life. God Himself isn't going to do anything to you because He knows you're ignorant. But, on the other hand, evil spirits will tear you apart. God will remove his edge around and evil spirits will have the right of privilege over you.

Once, God asked me to move to Maryland because He had an assignment for me. When I moved with my family to Maryland, I had no job to earn money to pay for our apartment. I found a job with an employment agency that would send me to different job sites every week. One day, the job agency sent me to a job site in Jessup for a week. At this job site, I was helping with recycling cardboard, plastic, and Styrofoam. At noon, the site supervisor called for a thirty-minute lunch break. All the workers would go to a lovely lounge room equipped with the latest kitchen appliances. There were many microwaves, toasters, air fryers, and two beautiful refrigerators where employees could store their food. The lounge room had many tables with four chairs around each one.

The place was well organized, and the floor was immaculate. Adjacent to my table was a young guy around 23 years of age. A guy sitting at my table asked him how his girlfriend was doing. I didn't get the 23-year-old boy's name, and he wasn't working where I was. His face went pale when he started talking about what his girlfriend was going through, with a hopeless look on his face. He was telling the guy next to me how his girlfriend couldn't sleep at night, and all her medications were no help. The doctors tried everything possible, and anything seemed to work for her. She couldn't go to work anymore and stayed in bed all day. Lately, the 23-year-old boy added that his girlfriend became suicidal, trying to take her life. When I heard all that, I felt compassionate, and I knew an evil spirit was trying to take the life of an innocent girl. At the end of the lunch break, I approached the young man to call his girlfriend so I could pray for her. I told the young man I had authority over all kinds of spirits and could pray for her girl to recover. At first, he was enthusiastic and glad to find somebody who could do something for his girlfriend to recover. But, when he realized that I was saying that I would call on God to heal his girlfriend, he became cold and reluctant. That was when he told me he and his girlfriend were atheists and didn't believe in God. They wouldn't take any healing from God. I was shocked, and my mouth just locked open. My brain went blank, and I didn't have a word to answer the young man. Then he walked away. I was at that job site for less than a week, and each time this young saw me, he would change the route or walk far away; according to the young man, his girlfriend cursed at God in front of her parents, who were trying to take her to church when she newly joined the group of atheists.

## 9. Lust in heart by looking at a woman or man.

**Matthew 5:28. But I tell you that anyone who looks at a woman lustfully has already committed adultery with her in his heart.**

The way this verse works is as follows. Suppose a man sees a beautiful woman who catches his attention and starts contemplating how to play with this woman in bed, the man sins. Immediately, on the spot, an evil spirit will enter that man to take him on routes of sexual perversion. If the man doesn't repent from his lust for the woman, the evil spirit will lure him into different sexual immoralities. The spirit will gradually teach him how to deprave from sexual immoralities. By the time this man realizes he is no longer what he used to be, he may hurt a lot of women emotionally and psychologically.

One day, I was far away from my wife in a different state. I was in a grocery store buying some fruits and bread. I spotted a woman who looked exactly like my wife in the grocery store. The woman's eyelashes and her lips were just like my wife's. Her nose and facial expression were identical. I didn't know how that happened, and my mind went to my bedroom with my wife the last time we were intimate. All of a sudden, I felt a different sensation go inside of me. I knew it was an evil spirit. I started confessing my sins to the Lord. I admitted my guilt. I was telling the Lord that I didn't mean to take that woman who resembled my wife to my bedroom. I asked for forgiveness, and the Lord removed that spirit from me. Evil spirits know that people, in general, don't like their company. So, they'll never come to you as an evil spirit, but as a simple feeling. They try to disguise their nature and purpose until they ultimately control their victims.

# III

# Behaviors that show the presence of the enemy

Demons are always avid of a body. Any time a demon has the chance to possess a body, he becomes active. First, it will give dreams to the victim that determine the type of demon it is. If it's a marine demon, it will provide dreams where the victim will see himself at a river playing with other people he may know. The demon will start taking away what's good in the life of the victim. For example, if the victim likes to read, the demon will gradually remove the desire to read from the victim.

# IV

# Sickness caused by the enemy

## 1. Anxiety disorder

Anxiety disorder is a mental health condition that involves persistent and excessive fear, worry, and apprehension. It can interfere seriously with daily activities. Anxiety disorder has earnest effects on the victim's life, with physical symptoms like trembling, restlessness, difficulty concentrating, muscle tension, rapid heartbeat, and problems sleeping. A little event in the victim's life can trigger ongoing worry and stress. Sometimes, it's a mere idea of losing a relationship or a sick family member. There are many types of anxiety disorders, such as generalized anxiety disorder, social anxiety disorder, panic disorder, social isolation, and avoidance of everyday activities. In all these cases, an anxious spirit causes dysfunction in the victim's life. The anxious spirit works tirelessly to make his victim miserable by introducing a scenario in their mind that causes the victim to be worried.

## 2. Depression

Depression is a severe and complex mental health disorder, and its cause remains, up to today, a scientific mystery. It's a mood disorder that causes feelings of sadness, hopelessness, and despair. Depression causes the victim to have trouble doing normal day-to-day activities such as going to work or to the grocery store. Some common effects of depression include difficulty sleeping, changes in appetite, and a lack of interest in daily activities. People who live through abuse, severe losses, or stressful events are more likely to develop depression. There are some known risk factors for depression, such as family history, unexpected death of a family member, job loss, divorce, or sickness. The depressive spirit uses an unfortunate event in the life of the victim to have access to the victim's mood. Then, it'll manipulate the victim's feelings and maintain the victim in a constant loss of interest in any activities.

## 3. Bipolar disorder

Bipolar disorder is a mental health condition that causes unusual shifts in a person's mood, energy, and ability to function. The exact cause of bipolar disorder isn't known, but some personal predispositions such as environment, genetics, brain structure, and chemistry are vital factors. Bipolar disorder has two significant poles, mainly the manic episodes and the depressive episodes. Each episode can last for weeks or months and can paralyze the victim's daily activities, inflicting low motivation and a loss of interest in life in general. In a manic episode, the mentally sick will feel euphoric, full of energy, or uncontrollably irritated. The mood swings always make family members uncomfortable, knowing not what to expect from an unpredictable loved one. Some days, the victim will wake up energized, joyful, and eager to do everything. On some other days, the victim will be sad, indifferent, hopeless, and downcast. The bipolar spirit afflicts the victim with all kinds of mood spectrum. The victim will become a prisoner of his feelings and will behave according to the way he feels. Doing so creates an unsafe environment for people around him.

## 4. Dementia

Dementia is a term used to describe a group of symptoms affecting an individual's cognitive and behavioral abilities. It's like an umbrella term for a wide range of neurological conditions affecting the brain that impact behaviors. Generally, dementia involves mental decline, difficulty thinking, delusion, forgetfulness, confusion, loss of the ability to think right, and much more. The loss of mental faculties causes the victim to become aggressive, confused, agitated, negligent, and wander around. The spirit of dementia creates chaos in the minds of the victims, causing them to become hallucinated. The spirit projects sceneries in the minds of the victims, who take them as a factual event.

## 5. Schizophrenia

Schizophrenia is a chronic brain disorder that affects a person's to think right, feel well, and behave correctly. The symptoms are various and can include hallucinations, incoherent thinking, delusions, disorganized speech, lack of motivation, and mood swings. The symptoms of schizophrenia can become severe and affect the victim's daily life. The victim will struggle to maintain relationships with friends and family. The possibility of holding down a decent job with people who display the symptoms of schizophrenia is very slim. They cannot perform their job accurately because of the constant interference of delusions and hallucinations. They constantly go in and out of the hospital, and medical personnel have no control over the delusions and hallucinations. There is no cure for schizophrenia because the symptoms are the effects of an evil spirit.

## 6. Phobias

A phobia is an intense anxiety disorder involving excessive and irrational fear of particular objects or life situations. These objects and situations are not just random but specific objects and situations the victims encountered before in their lives. Each time the victims encounter the objects or the situations, there is a reaction of an uncontrollable fear that causes the victims to tremble, have rapid heartbeat, have nausea, and feel dizzy. These symptoms can severely impact the victims' lives, making them stay away from some objects and situations. There are many types of phobia, each with a deep agent of interference. People have a phobia of a specific object, such as spiders (arachnophobia), needles (trypanophobia), snakes (ophidiophobia), crabs (kabourophobia), lobsters (ailurophobia), and much more like ablutophobia, taurophobia, agoraphobia.

# 7. Eating disorder like Anorexia and Bulimia

Anorexia nervosa is a dangerous eating disorder that causes an intense fear of gaining weight, a distorted self-image, and a refusal to maintain a healthy diet. The majority of people suffering from anorexia nervosa are females who are excessively preoccupied with thoughts of food, weight, or body shape. Individuals with anorexia nervosa engage in restrictive eating behavior and excessive physical exercise with the sole purpose of losing weight. Even if the victims are underweight, they fight harder to lose more weight. Constantly, there is a voice telling them that they are still overweight and continue to lose weight until they die. We have two types of anorexia nervosa, which are the restrictive anorexia and the binge-purge. Restrictive anorexia causes people to severely limit the amount of food consumption and starve to death. The binge-purge leads individuals to eat a good amount of food and, right after, vomit everything they have consumed.

These mental sicknesses affect primarily teenage girls who idolize a famous actress or movie star. The adolescent girls play the image of their favorite star in their heads until an evil spirit breaks through to help the girls get to where they want to be. The evil spirit will start telling the girls to lose weight whenever it has access to their minds. It will tell them constantly to lose weight, even if they are already underweight, to get the shape and beauty of their favorite actress. The scenario will continue until the girls will die if help doesn't come sooner.

# 8. Autism

Autism, or autism spectrum disorder, refers to a broad range of conditions that affect communication and social interaction skills. It is a developmental disorder that generally surfaces between one and two years of age and is characterized by challenges in social skills, communication, behaviors, learning, and thinking. It is a lifelong condition in which the victims require significant support in their daily activities. Autism affects people differently and with different intensities. Some have fewer challenges, and others have excessive challenges throughout their lives. The demons of autism attack the babies while they are still fetuses in the womb of their mother. The mothers contribute a lot to granting access to evil spirits to inflict developmental damage on the fetuses. Sometimes, the family history holds clues about the ill-development of a child. At other times, the environment contributes significantly. It is an environment with a lot of cursing, verbal abuse, drinking, smoking, anger, and much more.

# 9. Asthma (COPD)

Asthma is a chronic respiratory condition that affects the lungs and airways. It causes inflammation, constriction, and difficulty breathing. When breathing out, asthma causes frequent whistling sounds, and shortness of breath can become severe. Medical professionals cannot cure asthma. However, its symptoms can be costly and controlled by medications. The causes of asthma are still unknown, but some factors can trigger episodes of asthma attacks. Physical activities, stress, allergens, and pollution can cause asthma attacks. The spirit of asthma causes the chest tightness and breathlessness of the victims. Asthma spirit is a bustling spirit that controls a handful of people. The purpose of the asthma spirit is to cause misery in the lives of its victims. It moves at the speed of the light, going from victim to victim, causing suffering.

## 10. Arthritis

Arthritis is a disease that causes inflammation in one or more joints, resulting in pain and stiffness. The main symptoms are joint pain and stiffness, which worsen as people age. It is believed that rheumatoid arthritis causes the immune system to attack the joints, beginning with the lining of joints. The cartilage breaks down, causing pain in the joints that attach the fingers to the hands and the toes to the feet. The most common types of arthritis are osteoarthritis and rheumatoid arthritis. Common effects of arthritis include pain, swelling, stiffness, and range of motion. Arthritis can lead to permanent joint damage and deformation. Like the asthma spirit, the arthritis spirit controls many people that it visits in one day to cause pain and suffering.

## 11. Lupus

Lupus is a disease that occurs when the immune system attacks its own tissues and organs. The immune system, which is supposed to protect the body from infection and disease, starts attacking body cells, tissues, and organs. It is an autoimmune disease that causes inflammation in different body parts, including the skin, kidneys, blood cells, brain, heart, lungs, and more. Lupus symptoms include joint pain, swelling, fatigue, fever, chest pain, hair loss, and skin rashes. The apparent signs of Lupus are a facial rash resembling a butterfly's wings forming across both cheeks. Lupus is tricky to diagnose because its signs and symptoms mimic signs and symptoms of other diseases. The spirit of Lupus causes a lot of damage to the body's mechanism to inflict maximum pain and suffering. All these spiritual diseases can attack Christians and non-Christian alike, as long as we open the door and give access to the enemy.

# 12. Epilepsy

Epilepsy is a chronic neurological disorder characterized by groups of nerve cells, or neurons, sending wrong signals in the brain and causing seizures. A seizure is a sudden behavior alteration due to a momentary change in the tiny electrical impulses' orderly pattern. In the brain, neurons generate electrical and chemical signals in an orderly manner that act on other tissues, organs, and muscles to produce human thoughts, feelings, and movements. When a disturbance occurs in the brain, where the neurons send many signals simultaneously and much faster than usual, seizures occur. Usually, epileptics recover quickly after a seizure, but for some others, it may take up to hours. After a seizure, people with epilepsy experience symptoms like headaches, confusion, memory loss, mood changes, and they feel tired, sleepy, weak, confused, and more.

The demon of epilepsy is a potent evil spirit, and rare are pastors and men of God who have authority over the epilepsy spirit. The only man of God I know now who has an unwavering authority on the epilepsy spirit is Evangelist Paul

Dodji Noumonvi, the leader of the "Jesus Is the Solution" prayer camp. Other men of God may be out there with authority over epilepsy demons, but I don't know them. Even in the "Jesus Is the Solution" prayer camp, it takes weeks for the victims to be completely free from the epilepsy demons. If you think you have epilepsy, please follow the ministry of the Evangelist Paul Dodji Noumonvi on YouTube or visit his prayer camp.

# V

# Victory is always on our side

**John 16:33**

**I have told you these things, so that in me you may have peace. In this world you will have trouble. But take heart! I have overcome the world.**

Every Christian is supposed to defeat every witch and wizard who starts a spiritual war against him. It's a battle that God has already won for us on the cross of Jesus. If it comes to pass that a Christian is defeated, it means that the Christian hasn't followed the guidance of the Holy Spirit. It's very imperial in the spiritual warfare with witchcraft that the child of God relies on the Spirit of God for a lead. God never goes to war and gets defeated. It has never happened before, and it'll never happen. If there is defeat, it's a sign that God hasn't been in the fight.

I mentored two pastors in two different countries in Africa. One of them, whom I would call pastor Ben, sent me a photo of his church under a tree. He added that the property's landlord took the facility of his church after a legal procedure.

25

He was devasted that the number of church members was decreasing every Sunday. He didn't know what to do to convince the members to stay. I was upset with him because he didn't let me know the situation until the worst happened. So, I ordered him three days of fasting and prayer to ask the Lord the root cause of his problem. I told him there must be an altar somewhere accusing him of mishandling the church tithe. He needed to go to God in prayer to find out the issue. Pastor Ben sent a detailed voice message three weeks later of his three days of fasting, no food and no water. He said he had a clear and vivid dream. In the dream, he saw that he was preaching in his church. The church was full of enthusiastic people. In the middle of his preaching, he saw his Uncle Frank coming to the church and sitting on a bench at the end of the church. He continued to preach. But, each time his uncle in the back said Amen to his preaching, a group of five or six members would take their purses and exit the church. Each time his uncle uttered a word, people left until the church became empty. Then, pastor Ben woke up out of his dream. He was confused and didn't understand the dream. Pastor Ben's uncle was a mason and a wizard. I was like, "Are you out of your mind"? How come, you didn't know you were in a battle with the witchcraft? He was on the battlefield but didn't realize it until he was defeated. He saw himself defeated on the battle-ground, and that was when he realized something was wrong. Pastor Ben was on the battleground, but he wasn't fighting, and his enemy overcome. The Holy Spirit tried everything to get him aware of his combat, but pastor Ben was nonchalant. Undoubtedly, the Holy Spirit woke him up many times to pray, and he didn't obey. The Holy Spirit quickened in his spirit to have an intercession prayer before church started, but he didn't obey. The Holy Spirit just left him alone and watched him.

The cause of all spiritual defeat is disobedience to the Holy Spirit. Every disobedience to the voice of the Holy Spirit is a sin against God. Most of the time, the Spirit of God speaks in a soft voice that is very easy to confuse with our thoughts. That is the same voice He used to speak to the Apostles in the early church, and it's the same voice He uses today. The Christian must learn to be sensible to the soft voice of the Holy Spirit.

Three weeks later, Pastor Ben told me he had found the land he wanted to purchase for his church. He didn't have the money and wanted me to come with half of the sales price. I sent him a frightening message. I said that he was wrong. Even if I gave him the total value of the land, he was still going to fail. He was giving me a recipe for failure. Pastor Ben's prominent failure was two-fold.

## A. First Fold with the Spirit of God

Pastor Ben disobeyed the Spirit of God, which caused his church to be taken from him. He didn't obey the voice of the Holy Spirit. He was living in sin to the Holy Spirit and wanted to adventure in a new project for God.

It doesn't work like that with God. Pastor Ben has to apologize, confess all his sins to the Holy Spirit, and earnestly repent for not being sensible enough to the Spirit of God. He needs at least three weeks of confessing his sins of disobedience and asking for forgiveness. After repentance and confession, he can start asking God what He wants him to do. God is the one who assigns duties and positions to people in the body of Christ. Pastor Ben has to ask God what to do now and where to go until he receives new guidance.

## B. Second Fold with the witchcraft

His progress isn't sure as long as a Christian has a witch or a wizard in his family. A witch in a family controls the well-being of everyone in the family. A witch doesn't allow anyone in her family to rise above her. Every day, a witch monitors the stars of everyone in her family. The witch will manipulate and influence the star of every member of her family, whether close or distant family members. Witches and wizards don't accept anyone in their family to rise above them. If a family member is trying to shine brighter than them, they'll do everything to bring that family member down. They'll attack the family member's business or all sources of income. Or they'll attack the family member's health by injecting an incurable sickness into his body. They do all kinds of dreadful things to people close to them. They do all imaginable stuff to people who are dear to them for the sake of having control over people's destinies. They don't care about family ties. Whether you're their brother or mother or a favorite child or a lover, they'll destroy you and still go to a pity party for you. They can be the author of your misfortune, but they can come around to offer you comfort or give you condolences for your loss. They're evil people to be around.

# VI

# How do you know you are under a witchcraft attack?

Generally, there are two phases to witchcraft attacks. There is a preliminary phase that I call the "Introduction liaison." During this phase, the witch tries to establish a connection with you. When the liaison is established, she will move onto the "Attack phase," which consists of introducing an object or sickness into your body.

## A. Introduction Liaison

When a witch decides to attach, she must establish a link between you two. First, she will do research into your family tree and find some close family members who have died outside of Christ Jesus. She will choose one of the unsaved brothers or sisters, father or mother, aunt or uncle who has already passed. She will use the image of that person to come to you in a dream. The introduction dream is very friendly. Most of the time, you will find yourself eating and drinking with a dead, unsaved family member. That family member will be amiable toward you in the dream, giving hugs or gifts. The witch takes the image of your dead, unsaved family member's photo to introduce herself to you. This scene can happen in the presence of other family members still alive. It must be a delightful gathering with people that you may know.

The introduction dream is very short. At the end of this dream, you will wake up in the middle of the night. Mostly, if you check the time, the dream must occur between 2:00 a.m. and 3:00 a.m. After this dream, the witch will withdraw herself from you and go to prepare for the second stage. The second stage involves different attacks introducing sicknesses in the victim's body. Remember that for the first stage and the second stage, the witch is in your room. The witch will use her spirit to come into your room by your bedside to give you the dream.

## B. Stage of Attacks

The second stage consists of introducing sickness inside the victim's body. The witch will leave her body, come to your bedside, and give you a dream in which you'll see your unsaved family member. The witch can choose or not to use the unsaved family member's image. As long as she successfully establishes the link between both of you, she can do anything according to her experience in witchcraft. So, she will travel to your bedside to give you all your dreams. During the dream, the witch will introduce an object to your spirit. After submitting the object in your spirit, she'll wake you up in the middle of the night. The purpose of waking you up is to link the object introduced in your spirit to your flesh or soul. The witch must link the object to your flesh. If she does not relate the object to your flesh, you will not know that you have something in your spirit. But if the link is successfully established, the victim will wake up feeling something in his body. It is why people go to the hospital saying that they have something bordering them in their chests. Doctors will analyze, but scanners will not find anything in the chests. The victims will affirm that something is in their chests, but the doctors will be inefficient before the sickness. Every effort the doctors will make will be in vain. The object is in the victims' spirit, not in their flesh.

A brother in Christ came to see me one day after church. When he pulled up his pants, there was a bleeding spot on his left leg. He woke up in the morning and realized his left leg was itching. The more he scratched the leg, the more intense the itching became. The blood was coming out, but the itching persisted. I asked him if he had a weird dream the night before the itching started. He went over to give me an account of all the dreams he was having. He was having nightmares about dead people in his family. Most of the people he saw in his dreams didn't know the Lord Jesus before their death. I taught this brother not to use his fingernails to scratch the leg. Instead, he used the palm of his hand to rub the itching leg.

Talking about rubbing a body part, it's essential to me to point out a special attack where rubbing is the only way out. Generally, witches use a technique to kill their victims. The method consists of the witch coming to the victim when the person is showering. The witch will study the times her victim takes a shower every day. She'll make sure of the time to come and find the victim in the shower. So, she'll come out of her body and attack the victim when taking a shower.

She'll get hold of the spiritual neck of the victim and twist it hard one time. Instantly, the victim will feel severe pain in his neck. The victim will want to remove the pain in the neck by shaking his neck and head until damaging his own spine cord. The purpose of the neck attack is to cause the victim to kill himself by trying to remove the pain. The solution to the neck attack is to use the palm of your hand to rub the neck and pray to God to remove the pain. Rub the place gently in prayer, asking the Holy Spirit to take away the pain. You have to be continuously in prayer until the Holy Spirit removes the pain from your neck. This technique is used in witchcraft to kill a lot of people.

My former boss did it to me while I was showering to go to work. He knew the time I got to work every day, and he attacked me in the shower. I was rubbing my neck and calling on the Spirit of God to remove the pain. In less than twenty minutes of prayer my tongue, the Holy Spirit removed the pain from my neck. Rubbing the neck with the palm is the only solution to the neck attack from witchcraft.

Most of the time, witches use a principle of equation. If I inject this in your body, you react this way, then this will happen. If I inject an itch on your skin, you scratch the skin with your nails; then an incurable wound will generate on your skin. But, instead of your nails, you use the palm of your hand or a rag to scratch the skin, then the wound will not generate. A witch can put something on your seat so that your bottoms will start itching when you sit on the seat. The itch will disappear if you put a handkerchief or cardboard on the seat and sit on it. The itch goes away because the handkerchief or the cardboard has not been programmed in the witch's equation. Whenever you do something that the witch doesn't consider before she plans an attack on you, the attack is void. The attack produces no effect. Whenever you know that you're under a witchcraft attack, you should change your routine from time to time. A witch will spend much time observing the victim to determine the best attack. Whenever you realize that a witch is in your house, get out of the house and go to sit in your car. The witch will be blocked in your house aimlessly, and she will be obliged to leave. Why? She still needs to insert your act of entering your car into her initial equation. Next time, go into your vehicle, drive the car to the nearest shopping center, and get out. If the witch follows you in the car, she'll stay there because everything you're doing has yet to be inserted in the initial equation. In 70% of witchcraft attacks, Christians can overturn them. Only 30% of witchcraft attacks need the intervention of the Spirit of God to remove them. Only the Holy Spirit can remove some wicked things they throw at people.

# VII

# The weapons and the battleground of the spiritual warfare

## A. The weapons of spiritual warfare

The weapons we use for spiritual battles are not carnal. The weapons we use to engage in spiritual battles are spiritual. They are not fleshly weapons like pistols, rifles, knives, machetes, or bats. They are spiritual, and our physical eyes cannot see them, but they efficiently do damage the spiritual realm. The apostle Paul gives us a clear picture of a believer in the battleground. Before a Christian engages in a spiritual battle with the forces of darkness, he should ensure that he has all the armor of God. The day a person becomes a Christian, that person merges on a spiritual battleground. The new believer will have to face the forces of darkness he used to serve. For instance, a person who enjoys the ambiance in nightclubs before becoming a Christian has to battle the spirits that lure him into nightclubs. The nightclub spirits will try to seduce the new Christian to return to his old habit. Every spirit a person serves before becoming Christian turns against the new believer to bring him back into a spiritual servitude. After Pharon had ordered the children of Israel to leave Egypt, the same Pharon and his army chased the Jews to bring them back into servitude. The spirits of Egypt have pursued the children of Israel to get them back into their initial situation, servitude. If it wasn't because of the mighty hand of God the Jews would have to return to servitude. A person who is under the influence of the spirit of masturbation, pornography, alcohol, anger, or adultery has to battle these spirits after becoming Christian. It's a fierce battle that the new believer has to win to continue his journey as a Christian. To win the fight, the new Christian has to use efficiently the spiritual arms of God in Ephesians 6:12-17. In these scriptures, the apostle Paul compares a Christian with a Roman soldier on the battlefield. The armor consists of six different elements and the seventh is in the verse 18. With the Holy Spirit leading the battle, the success is guaranteed.

Ephesians 6: 12-17 **Stand firm then, with the belt of truth buckled around your waist, with the breastplate of righteousness in place, [15] and with your feet fitted with the readiness that comes from the gospel of peace. [16] In addition to all this, take up the shield of faith, with which you can extinguish all the flaming arrows of the evil one. [17] Take the helmet of salvation and the sword of the Spirit, which is the word of God.**

Helmet of **Salvation**

Breastplate of **Righteousness**

Belt of **Truth**

Shield of **Faith**

Sword of **the Spirit**

Shoes of the **Gospel of Peace**

## 1. The belt of truth:

In the Roman soldier's armor, the belt is essential. Roman soldiers usually wear loose garments and need something to hold their uniform in place. Besides, they have different weapons that need to be on their waist. The role of the belt in the Roman soldiers' performance is essential. It helps secure flapped uniforms to avoid obstruction from their clothing. Apostle Paul is comparing the indispensable role of the belt of the Roman soldier to the truth in the life of a Christian. In his writing, Paul writes, "Let your no be no and your yes be yes." Telling the truth is very important in the life of a Christian. Telling lies causes disbalance in the manner a Christian should use his armors in the battleground. It's why every time a Christian goes to God in prayer, the Holy Spirit brings the lies he has professed into his memory. The

Christian must confess the lies and repent to readjust the belt of truth. Each time a Christian lies, his belt of truth gets loose and out of place. The Holy Spirit will put it back in place after confession and repentance. If not, the devil will use the lies to attack the Christian. Remember, all Christians are on a battlefield since their conversion till their last day on earth.

## 2. The breastplate of righteousness:

The breastplate protects the chest, where the heart of the Roman soldier is located. The heart is the vital organ of the human body. Generally, it's made of tempered steel, stainless steel, or titanium to resist spears. A blow or an arrow to the heart of a soldier will cause a certain death. A blow to the other parts of the body isn't as deadly as the heart of a soldier. The heart of a soldier is what righteousness is for a Christian. The lack of righteousness in the life of a Christian is as deadly as a blow to the heart of a soldier. When God labels someone as unrighteous, that person has no part of God. A Christian without righteousness is a dead Christian. Righteousness is the act of being correct in a tiny thing you do. It's a central piece of the Christian life. A person can't live without it and still be a Christian. A righteous person is mentioned 493 times in the Scriptures, and righteousness is mentioned 213 times. Both righteousness and righteousness combined are 706 times in the bible. The number 6 represents a man, and the number 70 represents the years God allocates roughly to every individual to live. God expects us to live righteously every day of our lives.

One day, I was driving from DC to Maryland on I-295. On a stretch of the highway, the traffic was horrible. The traffic was crawling at less than 5 miles per hour. I was upset and didn't want to stay in the traffic forever. I got out of the traffic and took the far-right lane leading to an exit. At the point of the exit, I came back into the traffic, saving me about 30 minutes of waiting time. The Holy Spirit spoke to me as soon as I exited my car and parked in the parking lot before my apartment. "You have just engaged in unrighteousness, saving you 30 minutes". The image of me getting out of the traffic and cutting back into the traffic after pretending to exit, came back clearly in my mind. I paid a heavy price for that act of unrighteousness. The Spirit of God had to teach me that every act of unrighteousness or righteousness became a mountain in the presence of God.

With the collaboration with another pastor, we started a little church in the basement of this young pastor. We took about a year of prayer and fasting before inviting people to our little church. The Holy Spirit was touching people, and the church started growing. The basement couldn't contain us any longer. We found a place in a shopping center at the edge of our city. Although the place was a little pricy, we decided to take it by faith. Members of the church put money together to get chairs to fill the room. Before the preaching, we set up two baskets before the pulpit to collect tithe and offerings. Under a joyful song, every congregation member would come to the front and drop tithes and offerings in the baskets. One day, God opened my eyes while this offering time was in full swing. I didn't see the offering baskets but saw a long table without legs at the pulpit. There was the presence of God beyond the table. Every congregation member was going, one by one, to the front to drop down on the table tithes and offerings. Each time anyone in the congregation put money on the table, their tithe or offering would turn into two mounts. The tithes and offerings were turning into two very white and pure mounts. One mount was smaller than the second but was immensely beautiful and pure. While contemplating the beauty of the mounts, a man named George came out of the congregation. He laid down a tithe, which turned into two black mounts on the table. I was becoming anxious that the two black mounts might contaminate the white ones. But not. Another congregation member approached the table and laid down his tithe, which turned into two beautiful white mounts. A voice told me that George's tithe wasn't correct, then I came out of the vision. Three days later, the Spirit of God brought to my attention the story of Cornelius in Acts 10. That was when He was saying that every act of righteousness or unrighteousness constitutes a mountain before God. Our acts don't go away, but they become mountains before the eyes of the Almighty God. I was afraid and scared at the same time because I didn't know our actions constituted a mountain before God. What you do to somebody, whether good or bad is still before the Lord Almighty.

## 3. The feet fitted from the gospel of peace:

The shoes of the gospel of peace allow us to be ready to share the gospel of Christ Jesus with anyone around us. These shoes give us the boldness of sharing the good news of Christ. The shoes of the gospel of peace allow us to stand firm in the word of God and be eager to speak of the gospel of Jesus. In Roman 10:15

**And how can anyone preach unless they are sent? As it is written: How beautiful are the feet of those who bring good news!**

The shoes also imply humility and service among the saints. In John 13:4-5, Jesus got up in the middle of the souper and wrapped his waist with a towel. He poured water into a basin and washed the disciples' feet one after one. Peter opposed Jesus when Jesus got to him to wash his feet. But Jesus replied that the latter wouldn't have parted with him if he hadn't washed Peter's feet. At this declaration, Peter stopped resisting Jesus.

## 4. The shield of faith:

The shield is an essential armor piece in the Roman legionary. Generally, it consists of a wood framework covered with leather and cased with metal, either brass or copper. It is worn strapped to one arm to deflect attacks from the enemy. For a Roman soldier, the shield is a protective cover that covers the body against any shooting arrows of the enemy. The apostle Paul compares the Roman armor shield to the believer's faith. Our faith in Christ Jesus operates like a shield strapped to one arm of a Roman soldier to repel any attacks of the devil. The devil uses people to say something to demoralize us. Sometimes, the devil can speak destructive words in our minds to bring down our state of mind.

Here is how the shield of faith works:

An old lady met a young Christian woman, 28 years of age, who was praying and fasting for a fiancé.

"Are you still unmarried and living in your father's house?" The old lady asked.

"No, I'm going to get married pretty soon, and I'll invite you to my wedding. Are you going to come?" the Christian lady answered.

"Of course, I'll come" the old lady replied.

The devil knew the prayer of the Christian lady and wanted to use somebody to bring doubt in her faith. But the Christian lady utilized her faith as a shield to demolish the devil's plan.

## 5. The helmet of salvation

Making a comparison between Roman soldiers' helmets and our salvation in Christ Jesus looks strange at first glance. However, a closer examination revealed a lot of similarities between the two. In Roman legionary, the helmet is an essential armory element. It's made primarily of brass and bronze. The helmet protects the soldier's brain against arrows, projectiles, and missiles. Any attempt on the soldier's head implies eminent death despite the rest of the armory that covers the rest of the body. Just as a helmet protects a soldier's head from physical harm in battle, salvation in Christ Jesus protects us from spiritual harm in the ongoing fight between the Christians and evil forces. According to 2 Corinthians 4:4, our mind is the battleground of the spiritual battle between the Christians and the evil forces. The devil throws at the minds of the Christians many different thoughts for the sole purpose of bringing them down. Knowing and understanding that we are saved in Christ helps us a lot to repeal ungodly thoughts. When the devil throws into your mind the idea of putting an article in your pocket while you are in an electronic store, you'll say to yourself: "I'm a Christian, and we don't steal."

## 6. The sword of the Spirit (word of God):

The sword of the Spirit is a powerful spiritual weapon that Christians can use to fight against evil forces. It represents the Word of God, the Bible. In Matthew 4:4, Jesus shows us how to use the sword of the Spirit to combat Satan. When Satan says something to have Jesus do wrong, Jesus replies, "It is written..." Jesus quotes a scripture verse that contradicts what Satan wants him to do. Finally, at the end of the dual between Satan and Jesus, Satan abdicates and never returns to Jesus again. Jesus Christ utters the Bible verses at the devil, who flew away from him. For Christians to engage successfully with the devil, they must read, meditate, and memorize the Bible verses. They need to know the word of God from the front to the back. Any time the devil injects a lousy thought into their mind, they can be able to retrieve from their memories a Bible verse that opposes the idea of the evil one. By so doing, they will be able to speak the Word of God with confidence and power and overcome any adversities they face on behalf of the evil spirits. They need to be sensitive to the Spirit of God to know when to fast and pray. Fasting and praying sharpen the Spirit's sword and make Christians successful in spiritual warfare. Christians are the sole creatures who can wield the sword of the Spirit to overcome spiritual adversities.

## 7. Prayer in the Spirit (prayer in tongues):

Prayer in tongues is a potent spiritual tool at the disposal of Christians. In my battle against witchcraft, I constantly prayed in tongues to get direction from the Spirit of God. I became so sensitive to the Spirit of God that I could pray in tongues in my inner person. I developed such prayer from inside myself. It was an excellent way to communicate with the Holy Spirit without opening my mouth. Whenever a witch attacked me in the middle of the night, I would start praying in tongues from inside. Then, the Spirit of God would tell me what to do. Whenever I obeyed what the Holy Spirit inspired me to do, a powerful force would throw the witch through the window. Sometimes, the Spirit would say "Praise and Worship" to my mind. When I was executing praise and worship, I could hear the sound of something projected through my window. Other times, I would get off my bed and turn on my TV to a praise and worship song. When I heard praise and worship, the presence of the Spirit of God would come on me. The evil spirit that brought the witch into my room couldn't stand the presence of the Holy Spirit on me. So, it would retract with force that I could hear.

Instantly, I would listen to the sound of something projected through my apartment window. One time, I was attacked in my bed around 2:20 a.m. by a witch. The Spirit told me to leave the house, and I entered my car parked in the parking lot. Because the witch didn't consider that I would go in my car, she couldn't come in my vehicle. She was stocked in the house and left after waiting in vain. Another time, the same witch attacked me in my bed, and I left the house to go into my vehicle. She entered the car, and I drove to a nearby shopping center. I got out of the car and started walking on the sidewalk. Since the witch didn't input these parameters in her equation before coming out, she got stocked in the car. I was walking on the sidewalk for about 15 minutes and turned back to go to the car. The Spirit of God told me, "Don't go back yet; she is still in the car." Then, I continued walking on the sidewalk in the middle of the night. God gave me some ability and sensibility to sense the presence of spiritual entities. When the witch was touching me, I could feel the touching.

In addition to feeling any spiritual presence around me, I could see any spirit that moved around. I didn't have the ability to see evil spirits or astral bodies. I didn't have the ability to see them, but I could see their movements. When evil spirits were moving, I could see their movement because they moved at the speed of light. To go from one corner of a room to another, demons would move at the speed of light. Their movement in speed beckoned my eyes. That was how I could sense their movement and their presence.

Prayer in Spirit makes me very sensitive to the voice of the Spirit of God. The more I pray in Spirit, the more tuned I am to the Spirit of the Most High. I don't think God will allow a Christian who doesn't pray in tongues to engage in spiritual warfare with witchcraft. I rely heavily on the direction of the Spirit of God to fight witches and wizards.

One morning, I woke up to realize that a witch had visited me in the night. I didn't have a dream from the witch, but there was a surge of wounds on my big toe. The big toe of my right foot had a painful wound like a blade wound. I did my one-hour prayer in tongues and asked the Spirit of God to remove the wound. The Holy Spirit didn't remove the wound until around noon when I felt the need to use the bathroom. When I stood up to go to the restroom, I heard a faint voice to apply the urine on the wound on my big toe. I thought it was my mind talking to me. So, I went to urinate without applying the urine to the wound. I came back to my room and laid on the bed. About thirty minutes later, I felt again the need to go to the bathroom and urinate. When I stood up to go, I heard a loud voice telling me to apply the urine to the wound on the big toe of my right foot. I said to the Spirit of God I was sorry. I didn't know it was him talking. When I finished urinating, I collected some with my right hand. I applied the urine to the wound on my big toe. Instantly, before my eyes, the wound disappeared, leaving no scar.

A Christian should lean on the Spirit of God to engage in spiritual warfare.

## B. The battleground of the spiritual warfare

The major battleground of spiritual warfare is the human mind. The fight we are engaged in with evil spirits occurs in our mind.

2 Corinthians 10:5 **We demolish arguments and every pretension that sets itself up against the knowledge of God, and we take captive every thought to make it obedient to Christ.**

Evil spirits have lived on planet Earth for millions of years. They know human beings very well and can play them in various ways. They know that the best way to take control of a person is through the person's mind. The primarily combat an evil spirit wants to win is having access to person's mind. After having access to a person's mind, evil spirits introduce gradually and little by little their agenda. They do this individually and collectively. They can take many years, many decades, to reach their goals. If you had told someone in the Martin Luther King Jr. era that the LBTQ agenda would be legalized in America, the person wouldn't believe it. Today, it's a fact. The administration of Joe Biden is working hard to promote that agenda to other countries worldwide. It's a plan evil spirits have been working on days and nights for many years. Today, we consider acceptable or normal a relationship between man and man or female and female. The EWE culture in West Africa believes an ancestral stool can link a person with their ancestors. The ancestral stool can connect a person to his ancestors, who can answer all the person's questions or solve problems. People bring money or livestock to the stool; in return, they will receive words from it. Sometimes, it can be instruction on how to cure a disease or lead a home. But it's all lies because the bible declares that: **"Just as people are destined to die once, and after that to face judgment"** Hebrews 9: 27.

People who die have only two choices: whether to go to eternal damnation or to paradise with Jesus. They don't have the chance or the opportunity to interact with anyone in the land of the living. Instead, it's a game of evil spirits that hide behind the ancestral stools pretending they are dead people. Many people in the Ewe culture fall for that scheme and offer oxen and goats to the stool every year. Satan always wants to captivate the mind of the human race to introduce false beliefs. He infects people's minds with ill-effective imaginations, reasonings, arguments, knowledge, and thoughts to keep them captives. That's why some people embrace some horrible belief that will send them to hell. The devil has built a stronghold and fortress in their mind. The strongholds and fortresses resist vigorously to the simplicity of the gospel of Christ.

It came to a time when I tried to drive for UBER to make extra cash. I received a call to pick up a person in front of a clinic. I parked my vehicle in front of the clinic and waited about five minutes. An adult man came to my car, walking with a walker and having difficulty getting into the vehicle. I came out and assisted the man. In our conversation, the man told me he had a health condition that caused him to come to the clinic every week. Every week, his blood would get so dirty that he had to go to the clinic for purification. The clinic had a machine that could do the job. Once a week, in the clinic, they connected the man to a machine that recycled his blood by removing the dirty elements. The machine would take about ten hours to remove the dirt and rejuvenate his blood with oxygen. He was complaining that his insurance company was paying the clinic a lot. I tried to talk to the man to look for another means of solution, like Jesus, who could heal him. He told me he was an atheist, and he didn't believe in God or religion. I was shocked, so I stopped our conversation. The devil built a stronghold and a fortress in the mind of this man that he couldn't find a way to Jesus to get healed.

# VIII

# The center of spiritual warfare with witchcraft

A Christian is a living creature. A Christian has no communion with dead people. Anytime you see yourself in the company of dead people, know there is a witch or a wizard at your bedside. These dreams usually occur around 2:10 a.m. or 2:35 a.m., and you'll wake up. If that happens to you, please don't go back to sleep or sit on your bed trying to figure out the meaning of the dream. Stand up immediately and start praying, walking around your room or house. Don't sit down or stand still while praying but keep moving because the witch or the wizard is trying to pin something in your flesh or soul. Start praying in tongues, calling the fire of the Holy Ghost to consume the presence in your room. While praying in tongues, ask the Holy Spirit, in your heart, what to do. The Holy Spirit will quicken in your spirit what to do to overcome the witch or the wizard.

When I was in this situation, the Holy Spirit would often tell me to do praise and worship or continue to pray. I would start singing and raising my two hands. Shortly after beginning praise and worship, I would feel the presence of God coming on me. Then, I would hear the sound of something that ejected through the windows of my living room. When the presence of God came upon me, the spirit that led the witch to my room couldn't support the presence and would retract. Sometimes, the Spirit of God would tell me to open my TV to praise and worship. At the beginning of my battle with witchcraft, a witch gave me a dream and woke me up. I woke up around 2:10 a.m., and I sat on my bed. The witch was speaking to my mind about lying down back on my bed. She was arrogantly saying that she had no time to waste with me. She had work to do in my butt. All of a sudden, I felt the need to speak in tongues. Just as I started speaking in tongues, I heard the sound of an object projected through the windows of my bedroom.

We need the lead of the Holy Spirit to engage in a successful spiritual battle. It's vital to ask the Holy Spirit the tool you should use to face every spiritual battle. The Spirit of God knows the tool to use in the battle. But if it comes to pass that you have not woken up to pray to avoid the witch's evil plan. When you wake up in the morning, whether you can feel the object introduced in your body or not, you must pray for one hour in tongues. After praying for one hour, the Holy Spirit will take total control of your body. Then you must ask the Spirit of God to remove everything the evil witch has introduced in you. It would help if you said:" Holy Spirit, purify me, body, spirit, and soul. Remove everything the enemy has introduced in my body". Then, you'll feel pain wherever the object is inflected in your body. When you continue the prayer, the pain will dissolve.

At the beginning of my battle with the witches and wizards, I didn't know that I shouldn't go back to sleep after I had received their dreams. In the morning, I would wake up knowing that I received visitation from a witch or a wizard. I would start with one hour of prayer in tongues. After the prayer, I would ask the Spirit of God to remove from my body whatever the witch inflicted on my body. Instantly, I would start feeling pain in my right knee. With persistence in prayer, the pain in my knee will disappear. I would do that anytime I realized a witch, or a wizard had visited me in my sleep. I prayed constantly, and the Spirit of God would dissolve whatever a witch or a wizard inflected my body. Sometimes, my dream would be messy: no organization, clear characters, sense, or meaning. These types of dreams also come from witchcraft. When the witches know that you're aware of their activities, they will try to disguise their behaviors. When they give you dead people's dreams and you react with prayer; then they'll give you dreams that are messy.

One day, I had those kind of dreams. It was just confusion and nonsense. But when I woke up, I realized I had a cut on my big toe. It was a very painful cut that looked like a wound from a sharp blade. When I looked inside the cut, it was red and sore. My hands couldn't touch the area where the cup was because of the pain. I immediately started my one hour prayer in tongues. After an hour, I continuously asked the Holy Spirit to remove the pain in vain. I persisted in asking the Holy Spirit to do something to close the wound on my big toe. I tried many times, and the Spirit of God would remove the pain, and I despaired and gave up. I went on into my daily activities. It was a Saturday, and I didn't go to work. Around noon, I felt the urge to use the bathroom. As I was getting up to go to the bathroom, I heard a soft voice saying to collect some urine and apply it to the wound. The voice was so quiet that I thought it came from my mind. So, I went to the bathroom to piss, and I disregarded the instruction I received from the Holy Spirit. It was about thirty minutes from the first attempt, and I felt the need to use the bathroom again. As I was standing up to go to the bathroom, the voice came back very strong:" I said collect some urine and apply it to the wound." I was like, I didn't know it was you, Spirit of the Living God. I went into the bathroom, and after I took a piss, I collected a sample of urine in my right hand. I applied the urine to the hurting wound, and before my eyes, the wound disappeared. It was an experience that I couldn't forget in my life.

The Holy Spirit is the one who leads the battle against witchcraft, and you need to follow his guidance to be successful.

## * The Common Mistake of the Christians

A lot of Christians, even pastors, have dreams where they see themselves in the company of dead people or the cemeteries. They think it's just dreams. It's not just dreams, but these Christians are under attack from witchcraft. It's their responsibility to wake up in the middle of the night to counterattack in prayer. The Holy Spirit has already enabled them to put up a spiritual battle with the forces of the darkness. But they don't engage in the struggle, and witchcraft forces overpower them, and they become sick or ill. The Holy Spirit isn't going to do the fight for you. The Holy Spirit wants to know what kind of Christians they are. This is how He determines the callings on the life of Christians and the assignment He can give Christians. It's sad to see that many Christians will ask their pastors to pray for them because they are sick—a sickness they could avoid. When asked how the illness has come about, they'll say: "I have a dead people dream, and the morning I'm sick". The vast majority of Christians aren't conscious that they are on the battlefield and that they must engage in a battle. Because the struggle is at the spiritual level, they lose awareness of this reality. Christians don't realize that just because they are Christians, some people at their jobs don't like them. Sometimes, people in their apartment complex don't like them. Why? Because a faithful Christian becomes a stumbling block to every evil manifestation. They oppose bad vibes wherever they are without being aware of that.

Since I moved to Maryland, people don't like me in the apartment complex I lived in. Especially if there was a witch or a wizard in my apartment complex, she or he had to move out. The simple reason was that any witchcraft spirits couldn't operate when I prayed. When the witchcraft spirits couldn't successfully attack an individual they targeted, they would become furious. They hated me so much that they became violent and aggressive toward me. I moved to an apartment in a city called Laurel. I woke up one morning to take something from my car parked in front of the building I was living in. To my surprise, my car was covered with broken eggs. It looked like someone deliberately threw eggs at the windshield and on the hood of my vehicle. To ensure that the act wasn't just random, I checked the rest of the cars parked in the parking lot. Sure enough, my vehicle was the only one under attack. Although I knew the benefits of purchasing a house, the Lord never allowed me to buy one. I attempted a couple of times, and it wasn't successful. I would see in my dreams the apartment complex I should move into. That was where the battles were for me.

# IX

# My background and my spiritual warfare

## A. Background

I was born in a little county in West Africa named Togo. I was the sixth of a family of eight children. My mother had two children for my father, and the rest of my siblings were from other women. We were poor, but we had a balanced childhood where both parents were present. The first and the second older siblings, females, didn't live with us but came occasionally for a visit. Their mother, a businessperson, died in a car accident, people told us. I started an elementary school called Primary School of Be Gare. The school was located 3 miles from my home. My older brothers and I had to walk to school every morning, return home at noon for lunch, and return on foot in the afternoon. In the elementary school, I was just an average student. In my classes, I occupied the rank of 18th student out of thirty. Although I wasn't an excellent student, I always passed to a superior class every year. I had that favor that my teachers didn't retain me while many students in my classes got kept repeating the classes.

My father loved idols, and my mother practiced both Christianity and idolatry. She urged me to go to the Catholic church in our area and purchased a rosary for me. One day, my father returned home from his village with a troubling announcement. He said he consulted the deity of his village, who imposed a special ceremony for all his children. The ceremony was significant for the future of my father's children and should be held in Benin. Above that, the oracle insisted my father's son, Philip, should not attend the ceremony or get close to the village. Our two older sisters who didn't live with us responded to my father to tell the oracle to go to hell. They said they weren't going and weren't concerned about any oracle. My mother and father made the necessary preparations and took a trip with five siblings to Benin. They left me alone in the house. I was in elementary school. When I reached the secondary school, I had a problem. In my school system, we had three terms in one academic year. I always failed in the first term, and I would optimize my performance in the second and third terms. I wouldn't understand what was happening to me. I would become evasive whenever I started hearing the Christmas chorus in the first week of December. I would go to school, but I daydreamed when the teacher was teaching. My mind would be on God and the kingdom of God. But, in those days, I wasn't saved. I knew nothing about Jesus' redemptional work and ministry accomplished on the cross for the humanity. In my first year in high school, a close friend of my invited me to a church service in my city. I would change my mind whenever I was supposed to meet my Inoussa to attend church. One Sunday morning, Inoussa came to my house to convince me to go to the church. I couldn't turn him down and went with him after many unsuccessful attempts. It was a little Baptist Church in Ahligo where I gave my life to Jesus. It was like this was what I was missing in my entire life. I went quickly through the new convert class and the baptism class successfully. I was radically saved. I didn't give anybody close to me a chance, and all my brothers and sisters gave their lives to Jesus. On the other hand, in the Baptist Church, I was very zealous in every church activity. We often had doctors and great teachers of the word of God coming from the United States to lecture us. During our study of the word, I learned that the miracles in the bible ended with the apostles of Jesus. Any miracle performed in our time was the work of the devil. Our teachers fiercely demolished the gift of speaking in tongues. They argued that the signs and miracles were meant to establish the early church. After the first church was born, these gifts were no longer needed. It was the doctrine I was teaching our new converts when I became the Church superintendent. I was responsible for training the new Sunday school teachers to instruct the many children we had every Sunday morning. In those days, I was diagnosed with a gastric ulcer that bothered me so much. The doctor prescribed a certain medicine to reduce the pain until a surgical intervention to correct the damage. I didn't have money to buy the medication, and I was living with the pain in my left side. Every morning before nine o'clock, I had to eat breakfast; otherwise, the burning in my left side would become excruciating. I led a group of Sunday School teachers to whom I assigned a specific class every Sunday. I divided the children into age groups, from toddlers to high students. Every Sunday morning, I would go from class to class to monitor the learning sessions. At the end of each teaching session, I would collect the names of students who had problems to plan my visitation during the week. During my duty performance, something changed my mind set for the better. A boy named Pipivi was in one of my Sunday School classes and had a spiritual problem. He started having a crisis whenever the Sunday School teacher was teaching the word of God. The boy would faint and lay dead on the floor. With the help of other teachers, the boy's parents would drive Pipivi to the emergency room. As soon as the boy got to the hospital, he would recover before the doctors could ask what was wrong. The boy would return to his senses, not knowing anything had happened to him. Then, the parents would return home with the boy. The scenario repeated more than three times before the group of Sunday School teachers, and I realized that the boy was demon-possessed. Some teachers called me to say we should have a deliverance session for the boy. We informed the parents to bring the boy for a special prayer after church. The mother brought the boy into the delivery room. We had the boy sit on a chair in the middle of the room and the mother in one corner. Four adult Sunday School teachers surrounded the boy. We engaged in a loud voice prayer, casting out the demon out of the boy. For about fifteen minutes of straight prayer, under the rolling eyes of the mother, the boy was looking at us. He was not touched nor moved in any way. He was indifferent and just looking around the room we were in. Then, we decided to confront the demons one by one. Even one by one, nobody's prayer affected the boy. We came out of the delivery room exhausted and sweating heavily. The mother took her son's hand, went home, and never returned to the church. On that deliverance day, I realized I lacked something in my Christian life. I knew something was missing. I was the Sunday School Superintendent, and I was supposed to give solutions to any questions that would arise. Here, I was incompetent before a boy possessed with a demon, and I didn't know what to do. I was kind of ashamed of my role and my responsibility. That was why some of us came up with the idea to fast and pray every Friday morning. A handful of Sunday School teachers would join in my room every Friday morning to fast and pray. I couldn't fast beyond noon because of my gastric ulcer on my left side. It would bother me so much that I had to eat at noon. So, I would dismiss the prayer session around noon, and all participants would return to their activities. We faithfully maintained the Friday morning fasting and prayer for about three months. Then, something happened that took my life by storm. In the fasting and prayer, something came on me like a cloud. It overwhelmed my body, and I couldn't stay standing up. I was looking for a seat in the room but couldn't find it. Then, all of a sudden, the cloud was lifted up gradually from me. I realized that the last porting of the cloud left by my left side where the gastric ulcer was in my body. I was in a state of shock and unbelief. I didn't say anything to the other participants in the fasting and prayer. I said to myself, let me wait until the evening, empty belly, to see if I would feel the burning pain of the ulcer on my left side. I didn't eat, so I continued fasting until evening. I had no pain whatsoever in my left side. I knew God had healed me from the gastric ulcer because it was during fasting and prayer. I was sure it could never be the work of any evil spirit. I knew right then that our doctrine of God did not operate miracles or healing today was wrong and misleading. I would go to any fasting, prayer, and night virgins to learn more about God. The leaders of the Baptist Church finally became aware of the fact that some people in the church had embraced the charisma. We had a couple of meetings with the pastor and the board of the church deacons. The two meetings were meant to brainwash anyone who would tend to consider the spiritual gifts. The deacons, one after one, would use the bible verses to demonstrate that the early church's spiritual gifts vanished with the apostles' death. Any miracle in our modern days must be the work of a deceitful and malicious spirit. The two meetings weren't successful, so the church excommunicated thirteen members. My job as Sunday School Superintendent was terminated, and I returned the classroom keys. We, the thirteen members who left the church, constituted a prayer group. We organized a night virgin on Friday night from 11:00 p.m. to 5:00 a.m., inviting friends and acquaintances. After a night virgin, I went home and went to sleep. I woke up in the morning and realized the presence of fire on my shoulder. I didn't know what it was, but I was confident it came from the Holy Spirit. Less than two months later, the fire moved to cover my chest. When I was in prayer, I would feel the presence of the fire. At first, I didn't know the objective of this presence on my chest. I tried to pray for sick people while the fire was present on my chest, but the sick didn't heal. I knew that the presence of the fire on my chest wasn't for praying for sick people. The purpose of the fire was to help me discern the will of God in my life. It helped me to know what God wanted me to do and what God didn't want me to do. I would say to myself, in my mind, that I wanted to buy a car. If it were the will of God for me, I would realize that the fire on my chest would grow larger. But, if it weren't the will of God for me, I would realize that the fire on my chest would turn off. The presence of this fire helped me make vital decisions for God's work. It was the foundation of my walk with God. I would know what to do and what not to do. Another presence came on me during a fasting and prayer held in the house of somebody I knew. We were praying in a dark room of the house. In the middle of the prayer session, the host stated that everyone should raise both hands. I raised my two hands, and all slowly I felt a gentle fire came in my right hand. I didn't know the purpose of this fire in my hand. I used it to pray for the sick, and the sickness didn't heal. It was toward the end of my ministry that I understood the purpose of the presence of this fire in my right hand. It took about twenty-two years to unveil the use of this presence in my right hand. I will go over it later.

On the other hand, my educational life was prosperous too. I finished studying at the University of Lome and started looking for a job. I sent my resume to many organizations expecting to gain a job in my country. All my efforts could have been more effective, but I couldn't get a job. Finally, I got an interview with a company that offered me a job. I was excited about getting into the workforce. We were two people retained for the interview. But unfortunately, I wasn't offered the position. I was upset and unhappy with the situation. I couldn't believe that God didn't give me that job despite all the prayers I sent to the throne of Grace. I started asking God questions as to what He wanted me to do. I would ask all kinds of questions, but God would not answer. But anytime I asked: "Do you want me to leave Togo?". The fire on my chest would light up. If it had lit up before I asked the question, the intensity of the fire would have gone higher. But if I asked a different question, the fire would go dim. The intensity would decrease significantly, and I wouldn't even feel the presence of the fire on my chest. Finally, I decided to go to Germany. In those days, my country only had a three-month free visa with Germany. When I announced my decision to my prayer partners, they were shocked and were in disbelief. They viewed my decision as out of place because we discussed starting a charismatic church. Some of my prayer partners became eminent pastors in Togo today.

Everyone has a specific calling in life, but it takes time to identify it and live it. Before moving to Hamburg in Germany, God visited me in a way I couldn't forget. It was a clear and vivid experience but not a dream. It happened at nighttime, and I was between awake and asleep. I was coming out of the sleep stage to the awakening when the event of God's visitation occurred. Right behind my bedroom, there was a big fig tree shaking. There was a big wind that was shaking the branches and the leaves of the tree. There was wind blowing through my bedroom. All of a sudden, the doors of my bedroom were open. A bright light came in the living room through the first door, and the winds stopped blowing. Then the light came into the bedroom where I lay on my bed. The first light that came in had another brighter light in the middle. From this brighter light, the voice of the Lord was speaking to me in a friendly way. But my physical body couldn't support the presence, and I was shaking uncontrollably. The voice started talking to me in these terms:" I know you are leaving. I come to you in peace, and your body can't support my presence. I come to teach you how to fear God because you do not fear God". Then He gave me a bible verse in Romans, and the light withdrew, and the voice stopped. I sat up on my bed, going over the experience. I was disturbed by the fact that the voice was saying that I didn't fear God. I thought I was someone who feared God very much, even more than people I knew. Toward the end of my ministry, I realized that the fear of God I had was just average.

I didn't have enough money to travel to Hamburg, and I had to collect money from family members. Finally, I gathered the necessary funds to purchase the plane ticket to Germany. I was with an acquaintance for a little while to learn the system of survival in Germany. I had to learn to attend school and work to meet my needs. I met some Togolese living in Hamburg with whom I journeyed every day. I was sharing a room with a Togolese that I met in Hamburg. His name was Francois, and he had just moved to Hamburg because of the political situation in Togo.

The place we lived in was called Mid-Little-Land-Weg. It was about three miles from the train station. A public bus-linked the small town to the train station. The public bus would come to Mid-Little-Land-Weg every hour to take people to the train station. Punctuation was crucial for survival. The bus had always arrived on time and leave on time. It always came on time and wouldn't wait for anybody, even if you were the son of the Chancellor or the prime minister. The bus driver didn't talk to anybody and wouldn't answer anybody's questions. The driver was to drive the bus, open the doors to passengers, and close them after passengers entered.

My class at Luber-Strasse started at 8:00 a.m. prompt every working day. I relied heavily on the Mid-Little-Land-Weg public bus to take me to the train station in the morning. To make it on time to school at 8:00 a.m. I had to board the 7:00 a.m. bus. The purpose of the school was to give me a background in the German language and prepare me for a training school. One day, I missed my bus by one minute and had to walk to the train station alone. It was dark that morning, and the outside temperature was -12 °C. The air was thick, and nothing was moving. The wind wasn't moving, and I thought everything was still, and a dreadful silence surrounded me. The stillness in the air scared me, and

I looked back many times. I was the only one on the road. My fingers were frozen and hurting, although I put them in my pockets. My two ears were frozen and breaking in a way that I had the impression that they had been removing from my head. My entire body was aching as if the cold air was trying to seep the skin from my bones.

Some rare vehicles belonging to people who worked in the area passed me with their high beams on. It took me about thirty minutes to reach the train station. The train was always on time, and I rushed into a train card close to me without paying attention to the class. People on the train looked at me funny, and I realized I boarded the wrong train card. They didn't know the Calvary I went through to get to the train station. I got out of the train card before the hostile eyes turned away. I was late to school. As I walked through my classroom doors, my teacher said: "Did you miss your bus?" I nodded with my head. He added: "You needed to learn to be on time."

After the classes, I would work for five hours in a bank named Dressner Bank. The bank was located among high-class department stores in the city named Jungfernstieg. It was a very nice and beautiful business center where expensive clothes, shoes, suits, and belts were displayed. The Dressner Bank closed sharp at 3:00 p.m., and my job would start. I would vacuum the bank offices and empty all the trash cans. I would replace old trash bags with fresh trash bags. I worked with some other girls who cleaned the desks and the computers. I would also map the bank lobby and the ATM room. I worked from Monday through Friday and had the weekend to myself. I started to look for a good church to attend. I asked some people who indicated a church in the center of the city of Hamburg. I went to the church two Sundays, and I didn't understand what they were saying because everything was in German. On the third Sunday, I pushed forward my curiosity at the end of the church to see the type of bible used. I found out that the leaders were using the Mormon bible. I told myself, "You can fool me twice, but I would not be fooled the third time." I stopped going to that church and found another church in Bergedorf, a Baptist church. It was a spiritually dead church, but it still held onto the brotherly love of its members. In this church was a lady named Anke who spent some time in France and could translate the service into French for me. The church was full of senior citizens and a handful of teenagers. After living a year in Germany, I started discovering the true face of German society. Racism and prejudice were deeply engraved in German society. People mistreated other people for the sake of the color of their skin. A postal office agent got beaten to death by a group of teenagers just because he was black. People could read the slogan "Black people get out" at some train station entrances. In some restaurants, the German language was mandatory before service. Seeing these prejudices daily, I started asking God some questions. I despised my plight, and I wanted to know why I did God allow me to go to a country with this magnitude of racism. God wouldn't answer all the questions I was asking in prayer. But when I told God I didn't like my condition and wanted to move to the United States, He answered: "Go; I will be with you." I went home to get a visa and met Julienne, who became my wife in the States. The Holy Spirit invaded my spirit the day I stepped my feet on the soul of the United States. I was thrilled, although racism was well alive in the State, too. But the magnitude of racism in Germany against black people wasn't comparable to the one in the United States. After three months in Florida, I met my brother Julien, who lived in Anaheim, California. Meeting with my brother after many years of separation was a glorious moment. My brother's wife, Valentine, also was thrilled to see me. It was a happy moment in my life that I thought would last long. This precious moment of my life lasted only three weeks, and co-existence problems broke loose. I didn't understand what was happening to me. I knew nobody else in the US to talk to and ask for assistance. I turned to my right; I saw nobody. I turned to my left; I saw nobody. The United States was a vast country, and the people I lived with didn't want me anymore; what should I do? It was a very troubling time in my life, and no one to turn to. I turned my eyes to Jesus and started praying. One day, I was on my knee praying, around 5:30 p.m., pouring my heart to God. During the prayer, I got carried away and saw a vision of the Lord telling me to leave and move to Los Angeles. He had an assignment for me in that city to tend to the spiritual and physical needs of a lady He had his hand on. A week after the vision, I parked all my stuff in my vehicle and moved alone to Los Angeles. I rented a single room on Santa Monica Boulevard in Los Angeles and started looking for a job. I didn't have a work permit and couldn't get a good job to pay my rent and put food on the table. Finally, I found a job as a security guard in a jewelry store on Broadway Street downtown. The job wasn't easy, and I had to stand by the jewelry booths for eight hours to scare away any thief or robber. About three months later, I transferred to a supermarket in Torrance. Then I met a Togolese dud who had a three-bedroom apartment in Gardena and was looking for somebody to share a room. I seized that opportunity and moved my eyes away from the horrible lifestyle in Hollywood. My security job paid me every other Friday a meaningless check to cover my bills. One day, I went to Hollywood to get my check from my boss and went to a nearby Bank of America to cash it. On my way home, the Spirit of God spoke to me loud and clear: "You are going to meet the person about whom I spoke to you in Anaheim." I met the lady that day. She was a black girl, one year younger than me, and was living with her uncle in L.A., Lynda Woodson. I prayed to God to ensure I wasn't making a mistake. He confirmed that was the person and gave me a recommendation not to attempt to perform a deliverance of that person. Lynda Woodson had a chilling story she hid from me in the beginning. What I noticed was that every person in her household, where she lived with her uncle, was heavily on "crack cocaine." Her uncle, uncle's wife, uncle's son, and herself were all using illegal drugs. They would spend a whole night smoking drugs and cracking jokes on one another.

Then, they would go to sleep all day long. Sometimes, they would stay awake smoking for three days and three nights. Then, they would go to sleep for two days. This type of lifestyle was so strange to me, and I wouldn't understand that a person could live like that. Within two weeks of our acquaintance, Lynda got caught by LAPD police officers and throned to jail. She came out of the jail after four weeks to explain that she failed to pay some moving violation fines. Sometimes, I wasn't even aware that Lynda got picked up by LAPD police. My phone would ring in the middle of the night and there was Lynda on the other line. She would say that she was in jail for about a week, and she needed some money in her booth. I would go and leave her twenty or thirty dollars with the Sheriffs at the LA County Jail. I would never comprehend how could somebody waist her own life in a land of all opportunities. Whenever she came out of jail, I would tend to her need and take her to Noel Jones' church. It took many years before Lynda would be open to tell me the story behind her addiction to illegal drugs. Every time, she would get out of jail, she would come with the decision not to go back to her old lifestyle. It wouldn't take long for her to go back to the same people she did drug with. One time, Lynda came out of prison with a determination to turn her life around. She broke a glass pipe she used to smoke the cocaine. The next day, she called around for job hunting. Finally, she got an interview appointment in a law firm in the city of El Secondo. The interview was successful, and Lynda Woodson was appointed an assistant secretary of the law firm. The owner of the law firm loved Lynda for her humility and her ability to organize the file cabinets. She would receive clients with an exceptional politeness that caught the attention of her boss. Her boss was a slim white lady who had clients from over the world. The boss decided to help Lynda get back to her feet quickly. She rented one bedroom apartment for Lynda and furbished the apartment with her own belonging. The boss gave Lynda a queen size bed, a dining set, kitchen appliances, a living room desk. I didn't know if the lady purchased all she gave Lynda or got them from her own storage somewhere. Some of the staffs weren't brand new, but some weren't. Lynda was very happy, and I was happy for her. I was saying to myself this might be the end of my assignment. This happy moment lasted only for two months. In the third month, the boss caught Lynda doing drug with somebody and fired her. In that period of time, Lynda wasn't paying here rent either. The apartment manager confiscated all the belongings in the apartment to cover the unpaid rent. Lynda came back to the starting point at zero and she lost everything. She went back to the drug and back to start over. Her life was just roller-coaster. It was so bad that, one time, I decided to stop my assistance, my counseling, and my comfort to Lynda. At that time, she had some of work-clothes with me, in a way they wouldn't smell drug from her uncle's house. She had a couple of nice high heel shoes in my closet. I gathered all that and put them the entrance of my apartment, in expectation she would come and collect them. I was feeling like my counseling and my prayer were in vain. I got tired to see my effort thrown in a drain over and over. I made up my to cut short to the chase. At that time, I was still working for the same security company, but was sent to a new location in Cerritos. The Cerritos location was a big parking lot that I needed to patrol on bike. The starting time was 2:00 p.m. and the ending time was 11:00 p.m. from Monday through Sunday. On Sundays, I would go to a little church located between my home and my job place. The church on Sundays ended around 12:30 p.m., allowing me to make it to work on time. The Sunday following the day I decided to throw away Lynda Woodson's belongings, something happened that I couldn't forget till today. I came out of the little church, and I walked to my car as all regular Sundays. I was holding my bible in my left hand as I was going to put my right hand in my pocket to retrieve the car key, the Lord spoke to me. His Spirit seized me, and He said: "Open your bible". Instead of putting my hand in the pocket for the car key, I grabbed my bible with two hands and opened it. The voice of the Lord said: "Read". I didn't know what book nor what chapter nor what verse I was going to read. I started reading: **"No one serving as a soldier gets entangled in civilian affairs, but**

**rather tries to please his commanding officer. Similarly, anyone who competes as an athlete does not receive the victor's crown except by competing according to the rules".**

It was later on that I realized that I was reading 2 Timothy 2: 4-5. I didn't finish reading the two verses before the Lord started telling me this:" You are the only one to do this assignment. If you do not complete what I have given you, it will take me a generation to find someone who can". My mind went on the Lynda Woodson's clothes and shoes that I gathered to throw out. I presented my excuses to the Lord and promised Him to accomplish the assignment. It was a turning point in my life. Since then, I had never refused anything God tell me to do for him whether it was simple or complicated. When I came home that Sunday night, I took Lynda's clothes and shoes back into my closet. Three days later, I received a phone call from Lynda stating that she was going to stop by my place because she was starving. She was hanging out at some friends' houses and couldn't tell for how many days she was gone for. She actually came that morning. She got very skinny; her face had some additional lines going down her chin. Her lips were dry, cracked in small pieces and her clothes were dirty and smelling. My heart took flight when I saw her in that horrible condition, for I couldn't comprehend how somebody could do this to herself. It took a longtime for Lynda to let the lid off the deep secret she was carrying.

Lynda didn't know her biological parents. She was adopted by a couple in San Diogo who couldn't have children. Mr. Woodson was a businessman from Georgia and working in San Diogo. His wife who couldn't conceive a child was from the island of Hawaii. Mr. Woodson was financially secure and wanted to adopt one boy and one girl. Lynda was adopted from the hospital and didn't know who her mother and father were. Mr. Woodson loved the girl, but his wife Izabela was disappointed by the tremendous care that associated with an infant. Izabela detested the girl while Mr. Woodson poured all his affection in Lynda. When the girl started school Mr. Woodson would pick her up and take her and her older brother to an ice cream store on their way home. Izabela, on the other hand, was mean to the girl and blamed her for everything that went wrong in the house. Izabela had some younger brothers on the Hawaii Island who would visit the Woodson family occasionally. When Lynda turned twelve, Izabela's youngest brother started having intercourse with Lynda. The sexual abuse happened anytime Izabela's youngest brother, who was an adult at that time, came for visit. When Lynda tried to tell Izabela, the twelve-year-girl would receive beating and anger in return. Lynda became rebellious and at age fifteen she ran away from the house for the first time. She went to hang out with ran away teenagers in downtown San Diego. She was introduced to alcohol, drugs, and prostitution. She was introduced to a world of stupefying substances she had never known existed. She met different girls and boys going through the same abuse in their families. They formed a bound of friendship and mutual assistance in order to survive on the street. Lynda was on the streets of San Diego for about a week when Mr. Woodson, who was sleepless, found her. He took her home wishing to understand what was happening to his daughter. He proceeded to question the girl on the reasons why she left home for a week. The girl couldn't give him much explanation, if not only that was the way she was feeling. He took Lynda to his pastor for counseling and prayer which didn't do any good to the problem. Multiple times,

Lynda Woodson would attempt to ran away from home to be free. Lynda knew how to survive on the street more than being in a family environment. She could be on the street for weeks and months without coming home. Doing that, she ran into a lot of problems on the street. Going to jail was for Lynda a time to be separated from drug for a moment. The last time she went to jail, to my acknowledge, was for three months. She didn't call me, but when she got out, she took a Greyhound bus to San Diego to her parents. I wasn't at home when she left a message on my answering machine that she returned home to parents. Since then, I had never heard from Lynda Woodson till today.

Someone will ask why telling us the story of Lynda Woodson? First, it's to demonstrate how horrible it's for an adult to have intercourse with a child. Lynda's story has caused a lot of trouble to me in the hands of witches and wizards. My battle with witchcraft as a whole has originated from the story of Lynda.

Two months after Lynda returned to San Diego, the Lord called me out an early morning. He said: "Because you have obeyed my voice, I will bless you. Now your assignment is completed". About a week later, I was walking down Sunset Boulevard in Hollywood, and I was saying to God: "Lord, since you have approved my job, can I now go into ministry?" I was shocked that the Lord answered me on the spot, on the boulevard. I expected to hear from Him at night through a dream or through a revelation. I expected to pray about it for many days or weeks before receiving the answer. I didn't know He could answer me immediately. He said: "Do not go in ministry, because I have a special assignment for you. Your assignment here is completed. Now move to Georgia". I answered: "May your will be done". I didn't push the curiosity to ask what kind of assignment You had planned for me. The Lord didn't explain the assignment for me; He hid it to me. If He had explained it to me, I would have said: "No, please give it to someone else". I didn't know what was waiting for me in Georgia and beyond. I sold my car cheap and gave my belongings to the Goodwill Thrifty company and moved. The same week I landed in Hartsfield-Jackson Atlanta International Airport, that same week I got a job with company called Trojan Battery, Inc. I was sharing a room with a friend of long date living in Decatur, Georgia. Three years living in Georgia, I realized a constant attacks from evil spirits. Everywhere I went I had to engage in a spiritual battle, praying in the spirit unceasingly. Before I would go to bed every day, I had to pray a couple of hours. If it came to pass that I forgot to pray efficiently before bed, evil spirits would attack me. They would try to pull my heart out of my chest. It was a painful experience to undergo on behalf of demons. I would make sure to allocate enough time for prayer before bed for a sound sleep. I was going through a daily spiritual battle until something had happened to open my eyes. One day, I received a long letter from the association of witches in the US inviting me to join their group. The first sentences indicated that the letter wasn't random but a carefully studied notice. The letter stated that the group had found my star had changed in the sky, showing a kind of prosperity on my way. The star had recently evolved into a brighter state, and it was my star. The letter included all sorts of benefits allotted to me whenever I accepted to join the group. The group would protect me from adversities and allow me to get anything. I would make women fall in love with me. At this point, I was saying to myself: "I have one wife, and it's not easy; why will I want more?". The letter made me realize that God had changed my star in the sky after accomplishing my first assignment with Lynda Woodson.

I finally understood why evil spirits always attacked me, which caused me to be constantly in battle. One day, a pastor of a friend of mine invited me to support him at a wedding ceremony. They held the wedding in a church built in a cemetery. I went to the church well-dressed and sat in the front seat, waiting for my friend's pastor to call me. Suddenly, a group of evil spirits tried to overpower me. I started praying in tongues to repel them away from me. They would go away and come back in a way that I couldn't concentrate on the ceremony.

Finally, I was obliged to leave the wedding ceremony. Three different times, God saved me from car accidents. On each occasion, the Spirit of God would move me to see the vehicle that was about to hit my car. I would stop my car or move to the shoulder, and I would see the evil driver hit another vehicle. I felt like some invisible hands were planning something hurtful against me. But on every occasion, the hand of God would save me from every evil plan of the enemy. My mind went back to my school years. From elementary school to grade school, I wasn't a brilliant student. Although I wasn't the most intelligent student, I always passed my classes. I knew there were some witches in the community I had lived in, but they had no interest in me. I had a fierce freemason in my family, but he had never considered me. He did terrible things to people in my family; he had never ventured into my life. If God had given me that bright star when I was young, I would have died at the hands of witchcraft. The work of witchcraft was around me when I was a young boy, but God had preserved my life.

## B. My spiritual warfare.

In Georgia, I moved from job to job. I finally got hired by Fulton County School District as a French teacher. God blessed me tremendously through the teaching. I was financially stable, and I was saving some money in the bank for the first time in my life. I could meet my wife's and children's needs, and they had never asked for anything they couldn't get. Personally, the Lord met all my needs, and I was a considerable source of blessing to many families. I hoped this blessing would last for many years, but it was only for three years. At the beginning of the third year of my teaching career, I started dreaming of the same building repeatedly. It was an apartment complex with a green balcony where I could see men and women standing. I would see people on the green balcony, but I didn't recognize them. Most people I saw hanging out on the green balcony were white or of Mexican heritage. At first, I tried to ignore the dream, but it wouldn't go away. In this dilemma, I prayed to God to know if He had an idea about the place. I wouldn't say I liked the answer from the Holy Spirit. I wished I hadn't tried to know the meaning behind the dream of the green balcony. "That building is in Maryland; that is where you will move to," was the answer of the Holy Spirit. I said to God: "Why?". Everything was going well for me here, and I didn't want to start over in a state where the unforgiving cold reigned. I had only one friend there, Nazere Badagbo and his wife in Maryland. My friend and his wife lived in a one-bedroom apartment in Windsor Mill, a little city south of Baltimore. My wife was furious when I announced that the will of God for us was to move to Maryland. My wife was crying every night because she didn't want to quit her job. At that time, she just got a promotion at her job and was getting a better salary. I had to convince her that I would get another teaching job in Maryland and our lives would be the same. I called my friend Nazere to find me an apartment, for I would move my family to Maryland. I saved some money in my bank account for at least five months. My friend Nazere's wife found us a townhouse with two beds in Windsor Mill. The rent was twice what I had been paying in Georgia. I paid the security deposit and the first month's payment to secure the townhouse over the phone. Meanwhile, I started a home church that gathered twelve members every Sunday. The day I was announcing my decision to move to Maryland to the little church, I was very emotional, and I couldn't control my tears. It was painful to leave behind people that I knew well for an unknown land. On the day of our departure, I rented a U-Haul in which I threw all our belongings. I attached my Jeep Cherokee to the U-Haul, intending that we might need a dependable vehicle to start our new life. We left around 2:00 a.m. and had to spend the evening in Winson Salem, North Carolina. The next day, we continued our journey to Windsor Mill. Finally, we got the keys to our new apartment and unpacked our belongings all day. It took us a week to reorganize our belongings in our new residence. Our neighbors weren't courteous like in Georgia. Quickly, we set in our new environment. My wife got a job with the Hilton Hotel, and I enrolled my daughter Grace in Dogwood Elementary School and my son Josh in Woodlawn High. I was the only one at home looking for a good job because

I had some money in my bank account. I was jobless for three months, and my economy was running dry. I finally accepted a job at Sheraton Hotel BWI as a shuttle driver with a meaningless salary. I had learned since Germany to do any job to earn money to support myself and never depend on anybody. In this short window, my friend Nazere took me to visit different African churches in Greater Baltimore. Besides the Nigerian and Ghanaian churches in Maryland, there was a Togolese church on Route 40 and two in Silver Spring. There were a lot of God people in the land. I visited some in their home, and some of them also visited my family in our new two-bedroom townhouse. I became, in a way, angry at God. In my prayers, I asked God why He wanted me here, even though He already had a lot of pastors and dedicated men and women of God in the land. God didn't answer my question, but later, I would understand that we were born with a calling. Our natural characteristics shaped themselves at birth according to our calling in life. A man's physical ability and the calling in the person's life always correlate. If we could understand how God drifts people from situation to situation, we ought to be silent before him. He would do it in a way no one would realize that the hand of God was behind the seasons or the changes in a person's life.

God is in control over every situation in the life of every individual on planet Earth. Nothing surprises him. He deliberately chooses to intervene favorably in this or that situation or not. He does that every day according to His master plan. Our God is so magnificent that our mind cannot capture His essence.

Six months after I had moved to Maryland, a letter from the secret group that had sent invitation letters to me in Georgia came again. But this letter specified that that would be the last time they appealed to me. They had a great opportunity lined up just for me; I just needed to accept it, and they would do the rest of the enrollment on their end. Again, in this last letter were sweet promises of jobs, wealth, and travel worldwide. Like the previous letters, my wife burnt the last letter in a fire. I didn't know that I became the enemy number of the secret group of witchcraft. By burning their letter, I told them to go their way, and I would go my way. But for them, it was a defiance of their authority or power. So, they turned against me, and I was ignorant of their capability and evil intentions. The first thing they did to me in the following weeks was the introduction of a spiritual entity in my ass. They introduced in my ass a spiritual white tube that caused me to bleed whenever I defecated. They managed to put the tube in me one night. I was having intimacy with my wife. I was feeling that something was going into my ass, and I put my right hand there, and I didn't touch anything.

The object was a spiritual entity, and I didn't understand the spiritual dimensions well enough. Remember, my background was Baptist beliefs that stated that as long as a person remained a Christian, no witchcraft could affect him. Witchcraft could influence every Christian if the latter didn't, in turn, engage in a spiritual battle. God had already put at our disposal the tools to use to destroy any spiritual attacks, whether from evil spirits or witchcraft. Most of these attacks occurred at night, between 2:00 a.m. and 3:00 a.m. But that hour was when most Christians didn't want to wake up and pray. Some other Christians' problem would be ignorance of the spiritual realities. This group of Christians would be under a severe attack but would turn to medical professionals for help. They would spend considerable money and time in hospital in vain. By the time they realized their sickness wasn't physical but spiritual, their bank account would be in the negative. The Holy Spirit wouldn't do the fight for you. He expected you to fight using all the spiritual armor of God.

A year into my new life in Maryland, my friend Nazere came to ask me to help him start a new church in a city I would call Dalerock. He found an activity center where he could rent a room for church activities. He would pay for the room every week, which he could afford. Nazere came and picked me up a Saturday afternoon and drove about one hour to the place. When we were parking his car in the parking lot of the activity center, I raised my head. What I saw across the street from the activity center was stunning. I saw the apartment complex with the green balconies I saw in my dreams in Georgia. I saw a man smoking a cigarette and a woman chatting beside him. I saw an iron fence around the complex and a few cars in the parking lot. My jaw just dropped in admiration of the place while Nazere pulled me into the activity center. We were in the activity center until 6:00 p.m. It was dark when we came out. Nazere had invited some people for the first meeting. A handful of people came out, and we sang songs and prayed. My mind was on the apartment complex during the praise and worship. I wanted to leave the service and go to the apartment complex to find the leasing office. I couldn't do it concerning what was going on in the service. After the service, we drove back to Windsor Mill, and I was reticent during the trip back. It took another year for God to ask me to move to the apartment complex. After a year, I returned to meet with the apartment manager and requested an application. I submitted all the required documents, application fees, and security deposit. At that time, only one three-bedroom apartment was available in the whole complex. The available apartment was on the first floor, which I took and paid the first month's rent. I rented a U-Haul truck to haul all our belongings to the new location. The following day of our move, I prayed to God to ask if I was in the right place. He didn't take a time when the Holy Spirit affirmed the exact location. The new apartment was clean, but its smell was unusual. The apartment's backyard constituted a convent for witchcraft where many witches and wizards met every night. It had many tall trees with branches mingled into each order, and there lived a lot of owls. Every night, between 2:05 a.m. and 2:07 a.m., many owls fly from different horizons into the trees in my backyard. They would stay in the tree branches until 2:15 a.m. and fly in different directions. This occurrence repeated itself every night from Monday to Sunday. Many of my neighbors were members of the convent. A couple right above my apartment were influential members of the convent. In the second week of our move, the Lord called me in the morning with a strong voice and said: "Do not be afraid." When the creator of the universe called you to tell you not to be afraid, it implied that fearful moments were on the way. I answered the Lord that I was very fearful about where I would find money to pay the rent every month. I had to quit my job before moving to the new location. The rent for the new apartment was three times higher than what I was paying in Georgia. God made a way for me to find a job in a warehouse in Columbia. I would work the third shift from 10:00 p.m. to 6:00 a.m. Monday through Friday. Every evening, I would go to bed before 6:00 p.m. and wake up at 9:00 p.m. to prepare for work. Every time I woke up at 9:00 p.m. I would feel like somebody scratched my back with my fingernails. When I started praying in tongues, the malaise faded away. One day, it was around 2:00 p.m.; I was in my living room watching the news on the TV. All of a sudden, I fell asleep on the couch. I had a quick dream where I saw myself dead in a casquet, dressed in all black. I jumped out of the couch and started praying, calling out fire on every witch and wizard present in my living room. That day, I knew I was in the middle of a battle with witchcraft. When angry, a witch would give a person the image of the person dead. Mostly when the witch was trying in vain to hurt her victim. I intensified my prayers. My daughter Grace and I would often play in the backyard. One night, I was at my night job in Columbia when I heard a voice telling me to park my belongings and move out of my new apartment. I answered that I wouldn't move out, and the voice must talk to the person who sent me there. A week later, at the same spot at my job, the voice came back with a frightening question: "What is going to happen to you when we win the battle?". After a little pause, I answered the voice: "I don't care how many are you. You can't win a battle against that man". The following week, to my memory, it was a Saturday in the middle of the night, around 2:30 a.m., when the leaders of the convent surrounded my bed. I felt like some people were elevating all part of my body into the air. Suddenly, I saw a powerful lightning that appeared to separate me from the force lifting me. I woke up and started praying in tongues and calling on the fire of the Holy Spirit. That was how God got me out of the hands of the witches and the wizards who turned my backyard into a convent. The following Friday morning, something happened in my backyard left me speechless. I walked through the backyard with my daughter to get a book in the closest library. When we returned from the library, we heard cries of chick owls with their mothers moving them out of the tree branches. Many owls moved their chicks from my backyard's trees to a different city. Every night, meeting in the trees of my backyard had ceased for the three years that I lived there. The tree branches couldn't no more witness the owls' activities, and the Holy Spirit shut down the convent. My backyard was a convent for many centuries to conduct witchcraft activities in Dalerock. But when God decided to end it, no one could stop Him. At the same time, I was experiencing witchcraft attacks at my job in Columbia. At first, I thought it might be witches and wizards from Dalerock. Weird things were happening to me at the job, and I couldn't find out who was at the origin. It all started when I became the Second Shift Supervisor, working from 12:30 p.m. to 9:00 p.m. from Monday to Saturday. I had my computer desk in a bullpen on the warehouse floor. Every day whenever I sat on the chair assigned to my computer, my two butts would itch like crazy. I would scratch my butts until I would find another chair to replace the original. It happened every day until I started putting a piece of Styrofoam on every seat I would sit on. After that, the itches moved to the forklifts assigned to the second shift. Every time I sat on any forklifts assigned to my shift; I would scratch my butts the whole night. I started putting Styrofoam on the forklift seat before I could use them. Then, the issue went to the appliances in our lounge room. Anytime I opened the refrigerator in the lounge room, I would receive an electric shock through my arm. I knew somebody was behind these spiritual manifestations, but I tried to figure out who that could be. My mind would go to a wicked lady in the company. Her name was Maria, and she was mean to everybody. Then, things started happening to me at night when Maria would be at work. I knew from the bottom of my heart it couldn't be Maria behind all these attacks toward my person. But, besides Maria, no one in the company was a wicked-minded. Everyone in the company was kind and caring, and it was difficult to identify who was attacking me. Then, the attacks amplified. I was attacked at work as well as at home. At night, I would dream about my unsaved father, who died without Christ when I was still a young boy. I would wake up in prayers and walk up and down in my living room all night long. Sometimes, I would dream of one of my Middle School teachers who didn't know the Lord before he died. Sometimes, I would dream of the sister of my mother, who died without Christ. Other times, I would dream of a wicked army person who terrorized my neighborhood when I was young. He had never known Christ Jesus. I wouldn't know who was at the origin of these evil dreams. In the meantime, an evangelist came from Togo for a Sunday morning ministry. His name was Paul Dodji Noumonvi, and he had a powerful ministry against witchcraft in Togo. Under his ministry, many witches and wizards died in Togo. He had a prayer camp in Kpove-Togo where every spiritual sickness received healing. I took part in the Sunday service he held in Silver Spring. In the middle of the service, he asked the participants to stand up and he raised his voice to sing. As soon as he started singing, I heard the voice of the Lord saying: "This is why you are fighting for." Suddenly, a heavy anointing fell on my head and dripped down my two cheeks. The moments of my spiritual fights from Georgia to Maryland were moving as a parade before my eyes. I became emotional and started crying as I was re-living my spiritual combats. The anointing of that day helped me so much in my spiritual battle against witchcraft. At my job, I knew there was a witch or a wizard that was after

my job and my life. I would sense their presence next to me
whenever they wanted to attack me. One day, in the middle
of the exercise of my duty, they attacked my left side. There
was an excruciating pain on my left side, and I couldn't
perform my daily duties efficiently. I was praying and laying
my hand on my left side. By the end of my shift, the pain left
my side. At the same time, I realized that when I was driving
to work in the middle of heavy traffics, a presence would
come in to pressure my foot against the gas pedal. I would
feel like someone was pushing my right foot as to push me to
cause an accident. I had to call the fire of the Holy Spirit and
pray in tongues for the presence to leave the car. It would
happen whenever I saw myself in the middle of many cars in
a heavy traffic. It was a constant battle with witchcraft.
Another time, I was taking a shower to go to work. I felt the
presence beside me in the shower while I had soap foam all
over my body. In an instant, the presence turned spiritually
my neck. I started feeling considerable pain in my neck. I
started praying against the presence, calling on fire from
heaven to consume the spiritual being with me in the shower.
After the shower, I gently laid my hand on my neck, rubbing
it and asking the Spirit of God to take away the pain. It was
a pain that I could feel, but I didn't know how to remove it.
I just had to rub it gently and ask God to remove it. Eventually,
He completely removed the pain after thirty to forty minutes
of prayer in tongues. I prayed continually to God to reveal the
person behind these attacks against me. In all these
occurrences, I didn't know what I had done to deserve a life
of constant battles against witchcraft. One day at my job, the
presence came again while I was on my computer completing
my daily activities. I started praying in tongues, and the
presence went away. Whenever I stopped praying in tongues,

the presence would come closer to my desk. Then, I got caught up on my assignment on the computer. All of a sudden, I felt like somebody pulled my sex, and it became a doll. I went to the restroom to check my sex, and it wouldn't respond. I laid my hand on it, and it wouldn't react to get hard or firm. I went home and told my wife, and we prayed earnestly that night. It happened on a Friday. That Friday night, I dreamt, and I saw my manhood in the mouth of a black dog. There was no change for the whole weekend despite my and my wife's prayers. Monday morning around 11:00 a.m. I doze off on my couch for a few minutes. I dreamt my wife and I traveled to Japan and we rented a nice resort. We were holding hands on a long street where many Japanese couples were also walking hand in hand. In the dream, I felt my verge became hard or firm. Then, I woke up from my dream with the realization that my manhood had come back hard. I went to work at 12:30 p.m. with my manhood that wouldn't soften any more. Around 2:00 p.m., the presence came again while I was working at my regular desk. When I sensed the presence, I put my left hand on the verge and the right hand on the computer keyboard. The presence was moving from my right to my left, trying vainly to repeat the previous scenario. That very week, one of my female co-workers was pressuring me to have sex with her. I told her I was a pastor, and I wouldn't do anything like that. She worked the day shift and would leave the job at 1:00 p.m. after surrendering her daily log to my care. But around 2:00 p.m., the perfume she wore in the morning would follow me in the warehouse. When I started praying in tongues, rebuking the presence around me, the perfume smell would go away. I didn't know who was doing these things to me. On Friday of the same week, I came to work at my regular time, and the Spirit of God got hold of me. His voice stated loudly and clearly to my spirit that the assistant manager orchestrated the spiritual attacks. I was shocked, speechless, and in disbelief because he was the nicest person in the company. His name is Jason Smith. He was a hilarious guy in the warehouse; he cracked jokes on people all the time and called me all the time: "My brother from another mother." I couldn't believe that Jason Smith was capable of pulling the witchcraft attacks against me. So, I turned all my prayers against him at home, church, and everywhere I would have the occasion to ask for a prayer request. Fourteen days after I received insight from the Spirit of God, Jason Smith quit the job without giving a two-week notice. People were asking him why he wanted to leave the company so suddenly. He answered that he had a better job somewhere else with good pay. The general manager tried to convince him to stay, but Jason wouldn't change his mind. I was thrilled because I thought my trials and tribulations from witchcraft would come to an end. But I was very wrong. Contrary to my expectations, the witchcraft attacks against me intensified at work and home. I got all my family involved in the battle at home, where I organized a bedtime prayer meeting. One day at work, the presence came next to me while I was working on my daily activities on my desktop. When I prayed, the presence would go away and come back when I stopped praying. I got tired and ignored the presence to concentrate on my duty on the computer, with my two hands on the keyboard. In a click of an eye, Jason Smith turned into a snake and went through my left side to the right. Without knowing all the scope of what he had just done to me, I uttered: "Was that all you were bugging me for?". I didn't know the meaning behind what he did to me. A week later, I realized that my brain lost control of my renal system.

I wouldn't feel the need to go to the bathroom until the urine started dripping in my pants. The same thing would happen whenever I would like to defecate. The poop would start coming out of my ass before I would realize the need. I urinated two times in my pants when I cried to the Lord: "Lord Jesus, do you see what Jason Smith has done to me?". The Lord Jesus didn't answer my heart cry, but He was up to the challenge. The following week, something happened anytime I sat at my desk working on my computer. I would feel like anesthesia in my back, at the area Jason Smith damaged in my renal system. Whenever I walked away from my desk, the anesthesia would go away. Every time I was at my desk, the anesthesia would return and restore my sensation gradually. In two weeks, the Holy Spirit restored my renal system completely. I could sense the need to go to the Number 1 or the Number 2 before I would go. Then, in a dream, the Lord told me to prepare an anointing oil to spray all over the bullpen where my computer desk was. I purchased a bottle of olive oil, took a fasting day to pray, and dedicated the olive oil to the Lord. The following Saturday, I worked and aspersed the entire bullpen. Since that day, Mr. Jason Smith couldn't access the bullpen. I would see him coming spiritually into the warehouse and in different areas of the premises. He had planted specific demons in various strategic areas of the warehouse. He would come in to remove the demons he put in different corners of our working place. One day, I was at my desk, working, and I could feel an angel above my head. The angel would fly high over my head and then fly down low to my head. He repeated the low-flying and high-flying for a moment and disappeared. While that was happening, I asked myself: "Why are you all rejoicing up there while I am in the middle of a spiritual battle?". Little did I know that was the day Mr. Jason Smith gave up and vowed never to adventure my way. Since then, he has never attacked me neither at home nor at work. A week later, since I didn't see his activities any longer, I sent him a text message that read: "Mr. Smith, I want to invite you to my church because I know that God has a calling on your life." He answered my text message: "Thanks, my brother." I said to myself that he confessed that he was my brother in Christ Jesus. I intensified my salvation prayers on his behalf so that God might touch his heart and bring him to the cross of Jesus. A week later, Mr. Jason Smith sent me a friend request on Facebook. I told myself this might be the perfect occasion to witness Jesus to him. I prayed for three days and asked the Holy Spirit for guidance on how to win this wizard over to the Lord Jesus. During the three days of fasting, the Spirit of God didn't answer yes or no. I accepted Mr. Jason Smith's friendship request the following day and had a chilling dream. In the dream, I saw I was in my father's house in Africa. Outside of my father's house was a big, large tree under the shadow of which people would come to rest. In the dream, as I was coming out of my father's house, I saw a big, fine-looking ox in front of a big, long snake in the tree. The two animals weren't fighting but watching one another in the eyes. The dream was clear and vivid, and I knew there might be a meaning behind it. I started praying that morning to understand the meaning behind the dream. Without hesitation, the Holy Spirit answered clearly and with no equivoque: "You act like a senseless man. That man is not ready to convert to Christ." That day, I blocked Mr. Jason Smith from my Facebook account. The next day, he sent me a "Hi greeting on WhatsApp." So, I deleted his number from my phone. I had never heard from him since then.

In my house, I had been receiving visits from different witches and wizards at night. I moved with my family from Dalerock to a Laurel apartment complex. The apartment manager wouldn't let me come and check the apartment until my moving-in date. When I called to preview the apartment, I would get an excuse that it wasn't ready yet. Finally, the keys to the apartment were given to me the day I was supposed to move in. I already had our belongings in a giant U-Haul, and, with the help of some laborers, I had scattered everything in the apartment. Everything looked normal until the third week, when all hell broke loose. The apartment management was involved in witchcraft; the neighbor above my apartment was a member, and the one on my left also was. They all complained to the manager every day about me and that a lot of noise was coming out of my apartment. Sometimes, they complained they couldn't sleep well at night because of the noise from my apartment.

Little did I know my apartment building was sitting on a pit of powerful demons. The demons under my apartment were dark and sitting on dark horses. Demons on horses attacked me at night, chasing me to leave the area as soon as possible. I intensified my payer in tongues in the apartment. All the demons in the apartment left one after one, except one demon hiding in one of the kitchen cabinets. Every time I would enter the kitchen, I would feel the presence of a spiritual being. But I couldn't tell what it was and where precisely the spiritual being was. I continued praying in tongues aloud in the apartment whenever I was home. One day, I washed dishes in the kitchen while praying as usual in tongues. The demon dropped out of a kitchen cabinet and onto the floor. It was like a significant drop of water fell on the kitchen floor. As soon as the demon hit the floor, I couldn't see it anymore. I started to cast it out, but it wouldn't leave. It lived in my kitchen for a good moment. I told my wife there was a demon in the kitchen. She went in and came to tell me there was no demon. One night, it put up a fight against me. The demon went through my left side into my stomach and then into my throat all night. We fought all night, and the demon finally went out through my mouth early morning. I was very troubled by the situation and went into a three-day prayer, fasting, and no food or drink.

During my three-day of prayer and fasting I learned a lot from the Lord. It was an eye opener for me.

1. Whenever you have a problem with God, everything you do will not work. Or, let me put it like this. If God is holding something against all your prayers and tongues are void. They become inefficient. I was praying in tongues when the demon in the apartment went through my left side. It went into my stomach and then navigated itself into my throat. I was battling with this demon and casting it out all night, but it wouldn't come out. It came out the next morning. Everything I was doing wouldn't work until I fell asleep. Typically, every evil spirit around me runs away whenever I start speaking in tongues, according to the authority God has given me; under my authority, at the sound of my voice, every evil spirit should go to an inactive state.

Remember that all demons have an active state and an inactive state. I was speaking in tongues in my apartment, and it wasn't affecting this demon in my kitchen. I knew this demon had a mandate for something. I sensed its presence in the kitchen every day, but I wouldn't confront it. I knew something wasn't right, and the Lord wasn't saying anything to me. I told my wife there was a demon in the kitchen. She went in and came back a moment later to say there was no demon in the kitchen. I knew the battle was raging against me. It turned out that God was holding a grudge against me. I wasn't giving my tithe according to his precepts. My wife and I had a box in our closet where we put our tithes. On Sundays, we would take a portion of our tithes to the church we attended. We weren't taking all the tithes to the church. We were doing it this way for a reason.

The reason was that we had a lot of missionary friends who visited us from time to time. Every time we had a visit of a missionary, we would give him the rest of our tithes. God wasn't pleased with how I handled my family's tithes. That was why He unleashed this demon against me. My prayer in tongues became ineffective before this demon. After I came out of the three-day fasting and prayer, I took the box of tithes in my closet to church. I emptied all the money in the box and put it into the offering basket. A few days later, the evil spirit in my kitchen left by itself. I looked for it in the kitchen. I couldn't sense its presence anymore. It was gone.

2. The way we see demons and God's view are different. It's shocking to say that evil spirits work for God. There are things that God's angels can't do. They are pure and perfect in God's presence. They can't touch anything unclean and return to God's presence. God has reserved the evil spirits to do things His angels can't do. Early in this book, I have stated that there is no battle between the kingdom of God and the kingdom of Satan. There is no fight between God and Satan. God can eliminate Satan and its kingdom with just a twinkle of eyes. In Revelation chapter twenty, in the first two verses, we see that

an angel of God seizes Satan and bound him for a thousand years. Just one angel of God has the power to seize Satan and put a chain around him. The angel locks him up and puts a seal over him to keep him from deceiving the nations anymore until the thousand years end. We know that God has a myriad of angels to accomplish His will. Whenever I do something wrong, God doesn't send somebody to talk to me about my wrongdoing. He will send an evil spirit. It's not that God will personally tell an evil spirit to go hurt somebody. God will remove His hedge of protection, and the evil spirits will understand that they have the right to harm this person. When an evil spirit sees a person, the spirit knows if God's hedge of protection is there or not.

My essential duty now is the intercession for the Church and the kingdom of God. One day, I was tired from work and went to bed late. I woke up in the middle of the night, at my regular time, to pray. My eyes were still heavy with sleep. I told God I was very tired and couldn't wake up now and go pray. I would do it in the morning when I woke up. Then I went back to sleep. I dreamed that a very black demon with long nails descended on me. I jumped out of my bed, and the sleep vanished from my eyes instantly. I stood up, put on my clothes, and went into my prayer closet to intercede for the Church.

It happens so often that a pastor or a man of God is praying for a demon-possessed person, and the demon enters the pastor or the man of God. It happens whenever God is holding a grudge against a minister. The solution is to tell God that you have sinned, and you are sorry. Even if you don't remember your sin, you must accuse yourself of the situation and ask for forgiveness. If you are sincere in your demand for forgiveness, the demon will leave. There are two primary situations where pastors can't figure out the sin they have been committing. The first is mishandling the tithes, and the second is living unrighteously without knowing.

Toward the end of my ministry, I understood the goal of the presence in my right hand. I used the presence in my hand to pray for the sick, but they didn't heal. I knew it wasn't meant to pray for people, and the Holy Spirit had never shown me the purpose of that presence in my hand. One night, around 2:00 a.m., a witch came in I was on the couch in my living room, and I ignored her. A few minutes later, I felt her introducing a wire bar into my knee. I felt the pain, and I reached out with my right hand to remove the object from my knee in the presence of the witch. She left, and she never came back. Another day, I was away from home and working part-time at night for an employment agency. The agency sent me to a new location.

At night, I fell asleep in a chair. A witch came in with a spear she threw at my left shoulder. When I woke up, the pain was excruciating, and I reached the hurting spot with the hand carrying the presence of God. Instantly, I removed the spear the witch threw up in her presence, and she never returned. From those two events, whenever a witch or a wizard ejected something into my body, I reached out to the spot, and I could remove the object. God didn't tell me that I could do that for other people. Whenever a witch puts something in the body of a Christian, with the presence in my hand, I can remove the object. I'm waiting for that confirmation from God so I can help a lot of Christians. Many Christians are carrying in their body objects and sicknesses from witchcraft. These Christians don't know the origin of the pain in their body, and they go from doctor to doctor.

# X

# The vital role of the Holy Spirit

After I left the Baptist belief, I learned why my friends, the Sunday School Teachers, and I couldn't deliver the Pipivi boy. The truth and the matter is that when a person becomes a born-again Christian, they receive the Spirit of adoption. A portion of the Holy Spirit seals the new Christian and adds the latter to the body of Christ. This type of Christian has a minimal gift of the Holy Spirit. This type of Christian isn't sensible to the Spirit of God and can hardly receive guidance from the Holy Spirit. Thus, he can't do any particular assignment of the Holy Spirit. To be on an assignment of the Holy Spirit, the Christian has to be baptized in the Holy Spirit. The Christian must be able to hear the voice of the Holy Spirit, recognize the voice, and obey it. The primary benefit of speaking in tongues is that it leads to becoming more sensitive to the move and voice of the Spirit of God. When Christians speak in tongues, the Holy Spirit overflows from within them, taking over their bodies, minds, and souls. Generally, it takes about one hour of speaking in tongues for the Holy Spirit to take control of the Christian who is baptized in the Spirit. When that condition is there, the Christian becomes effective spiritually.

My colleague Sunday School Teachers and I weren't baptized in the Holy Spirit, and we attempted to deliver a boy who was demon-possessed. The evil Spirit didn't react to our prayers and intention to cast it out of the boy. That is why Jesus told his disciples to wait for the promise of God, the Holy Spirit, to come upon them before starting their ministry (Acts 2:8).

After I learned that I needed to be baptized in the Spirit of God before attempting to work with God, I was sad. Then, I prayed to God and asked Him why I wasn't baptized yet. He said to me:" I baptized you the day I healed you from an ulcer." Then, my mind returned to the day I was fasting with some friends in my living room, and something like a cloud came upon me. When the cloud was leaving, it left by my left side where the ulcer was. Since that day, the ulcer disappeared from my body.

Every Christian who has a calling in their life is supposed to follow the guidance of the Holy Spirit to accomplish the calling. The Holy Spirit must equip the Christian with the spiritual gifts corresponding to the calling. So, the Christian who receives a calling for a particular assignment has to work hand in hand with the Holy Spirit. A man can't do the work of God by himself. He has to lean constantly on the Holy Spirit, who will give him the trajectory to follow. That is why the Christian has to be baptized in the Spirit.

One night, I worked for an employment agency that gave me a third-shift job. At the job, when I finished my cleaning early, around midnight, I could go to sleep until 5:00 a.m. to resume my activities. One night, I was sleeping on a bench in the facility, and it felt like someone tapped my shoulder twice. And I woke up. I was the only one in the facility and locked the doors before sleeping. I realized it was the work of the Holy Spirit. I knew the Spirit of God was warning me of danger, but I checked around the facility, and there was no sign of any person. It was around 2:30 a.m., and no living creature in sight. I couldn't sleep because I knew a danger was hiding somewhere.

I prayed to God but received no answer—the following night, around 2:30 a.m. I received a visitation of a wizard. I was not sleeping and saw him moving fast to the back of a toilet paper box. And I fought spiritually with the wizard until he left unsuccessfully. He returned two nights later, and the battle was all night long. He was trying to inject sickness into my body. The Holy Spirit saw that coming and warned me to prepare for the war. There is no way I could have won the spiritual fight I was in if it wasn't for the hands of the Holy Spirit. With no baptism in the Spirit, a man can't be receptible to the Holy Spirit's moves and voice.

Luke 11:13 contains a powerful analogy that reveals a spiritual truth.

Luke 11:13 **If you then, though you are evil, know how to give good gifts to your children, how much more will your Father in heaven give the Holy Spirit to those who ask him!**

This verse shows how wicked a person is by nature compared to the excellent and compassionate God the Father. However, a cruel man rejoices whenever he gives a beautiful gift to his children. He is happy to see his children enjoy the beautiful gift he offers them. Although a man is evil by nature, he never gives a deadly gift to the hands of his children. It's common to see many parents buying new clothes and new shoes for their children. Some of them can buy new cars for their children. The way parents rejoice in buying a good gift for their children, God the Father doesn't rejoice in giving earthly gifts to His children, the Christians. The delight of God isn't in gifts like clothes, shoes, cars, houses, and so on. But His delight is in giving His children, the Christians, the Holy Spirit. God is happy when He pours out the Holy Spirit on His children. Why is that? Because in the Holy Spirit, a Christian can get anything he wants. Anything a Christian needs is in the Spirit of God, who can lead the Christian to his heart's desire. The problem we see so often is that Christians disobey the leads of the Holy Spirit. Some Christians who are well baptized in the Spirit don't feel the presence of the Holy Spirit in them or around them. When they constantly disobey the leads of the Holy Spirit, the latter ceases to move them or to speak to them. The baptism of the Holy Spirit is the best gift God can give a Christian.

**Note:** This book contains sensible information regarding the spiritual realm. I hope every Christian in the four corners of the earth have access to this book and read it. Since the day I decided to make this book available to all Christians, I started receiving visitations from witchcraft agents. I pray the Holy Spirit to be before this battle raged against me.

# Part 2

# Glance in the Spirit of God

# Chapter 1

# Why are there four gospels?

The church's story teaches us that there have been many more gospels, but the Spirit of God has selected only four for the formation of the Bible. The choice of the books in the Bible is the pure work of the Holy Spirit. Many scrolls were found in Israel narrating the life of Jesus Christ from his birth to his death. But why were only four of them administrated in the Bible? For a long time, I have struggled to understand why there are four gospels. Many teachers of the word of God couldn't answer me satisfactorily when I asked them the question. Some of them tried to go around the question. Finally, I laid the question to rest, assuming it wasn't necessary.

Recently, I prayed before the Lord, asking him to help me understand the book of Philemon in the Bible. The book is insignificant, but the Spirit of God has selected it for inclusion. During my prayer times, the Spirit of God enlightened my understanding of Jesus' teachings. All the principal teachings of Christ Jesus were according to a fundamental precept of God shown in Deuteronomy 17:6. The precept concerned determining whether something is true. It must be valid when two or three people affirm seeing or hearing the same thing. The concept could be observed throughout the Bible, from Genesis through Revelation.

Deuteronomy 17:6 states, "A person is to be put to death on the testimony of two or three witnesses, but no one is to be put to death on the testimony of only one witness."

Matthiew 18:16: "But if they will not listen, take one or two others along, so that 'every matter may be established by the testimony of two or three witnesses."

2 Corinthians 13:1: "This will be my third visit to you. "Every matter must be established by the testimony of two or three witnesses."

In this spiritual concept, the Spirit of God assembled the four gospels. A judge should draw the facts at the deposition of two or three witnesses, so the Spirit of God selected four gospels that testify about Jesus' significant teachings. The gospel writers testified that the person they were writing about was in the common of the living. They proved to us that Jesus was a person that they had seen and heard. Matthew, Marc, Luc, and Jean narrate the teachings of Jesus in a way to obey the concept of God in Deuteronomy 17:6. That's why we find the significant teachings of Jesus repeated two or three times in the Bible. Thus, two or three witnesses tell us what they have heard and seen concerning Jesus. The narrations of these four writers weren't under pressure, but they accounted freely for what they had witnessed. Nobody threatened them to write about Jesus, but they freely put together what they saw and heard in writing.

We should embrace these teachings as truthful because they are in the holy scriptures. Consequently, Jesus' teachings in the Bible are from him and authentic. When we read Mark's gospel, we realize that we have already encountered the same teachings in Matthew's gospel. Jesus' teachings in Matthew support Mark's teachings and testify that they are true. When we get to the gospel of Luke, we realize that the teachings are the same and sometimes more amplified. As we read through the gospel of Luke to chapter fifteen, we discover a new teaching. In Chapter fifteen is a parable that we don't see in the other previous gospels. It's the parable of the lost son. Even when we go through the gospel according to John, we don't see the parable of the lost son. This parable of the lost son seems to stand alone, and any of the other gospels doesn't back it up. This observation compromises the concept of two or three witnesses determining the fact.

We remember this concept is a spiritual precept that God himself goes by. If this is the case, why is the lost son's parable not backed up in the other gospels? Here is why the Spirit of God inserts the book of Philemon in the Bible. This small book is like the confirmation of the parable of the lost son in Luke chapter fifteen. The book of Philemon confirms the parable of the lost son. The characters in the parable of the lost son are spiritually the same as in the book of Philemon. The explanation of the characters in the parable of the lost son is almost the same as in Philemon. The interpretation is as follows.

## 1. The representation of God the father.

a. The father of the lost son represents the image of God, the father, through his immense wealth and the numerous

101

servants working for him. He is a wealthy man, and his wealth is beyond measure. His love for his son causes him to be on the lookout for his son's return daily. He expects his sinful son will return home one day. He loves his son but hates his immoral lifestyle. God loves every human being but detests mankind's immoral lifestyle. Every day in heaven, God expects every human being afar from Him to return to Him. God doesn't want any lost souls to perish and desires their return to the kingdom of the Most-High.

b. Philemon is an immensely wealthy Christian in the Colossians church. He has numerous properties and servants. Philemon is full of love and compassion for God's children, who receive assistance from him daily. Although he belongs to the Colossians church, he has a sanctuary in his house. Philemon uses his riches and love for the good of others.

## 2. The representation of the lost world

a. The lost son represents the lost world, where people live in darkness far from God the Creator. The people wonder about their sins and have nothing to do with God. They love their sinful way of life and have no consideration for holiness, and their conscience leads them deeply into immoralities. Although they carry some flares of God in their souls, these people are lost and sold to sin. God creates human beings in the image of God. God's divine attributes in humanity make a human being very precious in the sight of the Creator. Therefore, God loves all lost souls and longs every day to see the sinner's return to the Creator. God never rejects a sinner but does everything to bring the sinner back to Him.

b. Onesimus represents the lost world because he runs away from the comfort of his master, Philemon. He runs away with his master's considerable possessions and into the city of Rome to lapidate his master's wealth. Some scholars think Onesimus has taken Philemon's money for personal enjoyment. Other scholars think it must be the precious time of work. In both cases, it's evident that Onesimus has taken something precious from his master. This precious possession symbolizes the godly attributes the Creator invests in every human being. In his divine love, Philemon expects favorably the return of Onesimus. Every day when he wakes up, Philemon looks in the far distance, hoping to see his Onesimus coming back.

During his sinful pleasure in Rome, Onesimus meets Apostle Paul.

### 3. Moment of Repentance of the sinner

a. When the lost son finishes to dissipate his inheritance, he starts looking for a job. He finds a job that consists of feeding animals on a pig ranch. The lost son gets every week a meaningless salary and will get hungry to a degree where he wishes to eat pig food. But it's not allowed. In this state of lowness, the Spirit of God enlightens his heart to convince him of sin and the urgency to return to his father's love. He realizes the harm he has done to his father and the heavens. Deep in his heart, he makes a drastic turn to return to his father and ask for forgiveness. So, with empty hands, the lost son takes the journey back home to the love and protection of his father.

b. In Rome, Onesimus lapidates all the money he has taken from his master. He becomes lonely and resourceless, desperate for a means of survival. It's in this state of lowness that he finds Apostle Paul, who has been placed under house arrest in Rome. Paul seizes the opportunity to evangelize Onesimus. The Holy Spirit touches his heart to convince Onesimus of sin and judgment. He admits sinning against his master and the heavens. Onesimus accepts Jesus and decides to return to Philemon. The latter expects every day the return of Onesimus to his love and protection.

# Chapter 2

# The loss of Christian life

When I became a Christian, I received teachings from many Doctor of Theology. In the summers, prominent preachers came to my church to deliver powerful sermons—some doctors specialized in the Book of Revelations. It was intriguing how they linked the Book of Revelations to other books in the Bible, namely the books of Daniel, Isaiah, Jeremiah, and Zachariah. One time, a preacher used Matthew 10:39 to explain brilliantly how the non-believers would lose their lives. The verse read: Matthew 10:39: "Whoever finds their life will lose it, and whoever loses their life for my sake will find it."

So, every time I read Matthew 10:39, my mind went to the lost souls who were going to eternal condemnation for rejecting the Son of God. Until recently, after being a Christian for about forty years, the Spirit of God gave me a new interpretation of the verse. First, Matthew 10:39 didn't concern the non-believers. This verse was between two other verses that directly addressed the Christians. The first is Matthew 10:38. Whoever does not take their cross and follow me is not worthy of me. In this verse, Jesus addresses his disciples in particular. This verse concerned the Christians, not the non-believers. Jesus was telling his disciples the road ahead of them to follow him was a narrow path. The disciples should prepare to go through pain and humiliation if they wanted to please God. To be a true disciple of Jesus, Christians should go through self-abasement and self-sacrifice. This verse was in line with Romans 12:1, where Paul urged the Christians to offer their bodies as a living sacrifice to God. He was encouraging them to become holocaust on the altar of God.

The second is Matthew 10:40. Anyone who welcomes you welcomes me, and Anyone who welcomes me welcomes the one who sent me. In this verse, Jesus taught his disciples the transfer of authority he would perform on the cross on their behalf. He was teaching them that there were privileges that accompanied their calling. Anyone who persecuted the disciples persecuted Jesus himself. It occurred in Saul's life, who persecuted the church, and Jesus met him on his way to Damascus. Matthew 10:39 was in between these two powerful teachings of Jesus. So, this verse didn't concern the non-believers but addressed the disciples or the Christians. Mattew 10:39 says, **"Whoever finds their life will lose it, and whoever loses their life for my sake will find it."** it carried a more profound meaning or was hiding a principle in the kingdom of God. The principle behind the verse was that anytime God offered as a gift to a Christian, God expected that gift to serve as a blessing to others. Throughout the gospels, we saw how God dealt with servants who hid their talents in the ground. God treated severely those kinds of servants who wouldn't multiply their abilities to the benefit of others. If God blessed a person with riches, God expected that rich man to utilize his wealth for God's purpose. If God blessed someone with great intelligence, God expected the intelligence to serve His purpose. In Revelations 4:10, the twenty-four elders laid down the crown God gave them. They used their crown to worship God on his throne of majesty, saying, **"You are worthy, our Lord and God, to receive glory and honor and power, for you created all things, and by your will, they were created and had their being."**

The principle of returning to God what He has given to His children applies also to the Christian life. When a person becomes born-again, God expects the new Christian to surrender his new life in Christ to God. In return, God will reorient the life of these new converts to Christianity into a new environment with a call and purpose. But if the Christian refuses to surrender his new life to God, the Christian will lose the new life orientation that God wants to give him. If the Christian refuses to offer his life in Christ as a living sacrifice, the Christian will lose the life God has intended for him. If you give God your poor shoes, He'll give you better shoes. God will provide you with a new car if you give Him your old car. If you give Him your life, He'll make it better for you. Many Christians live lives that God hasn't intended for them just because they refuse to surrender their life to God. In the gospel, Jesus tells his disciples, **"Very truly, I tell you that unless a kernel of wheat falls to the ground and dies, it remains only a single seed. But if it dies, it produces many seeds."** If a Christian doesn't die to himself, he can't produce spiritual fruits. Many Christians live in the daily struggle like the non-believers, and they've never experienced the love of God. These Christians go to church every Sunday, and their praise and worship in church are the experience with God they know. They learn in church that God is loving, powerful, and compassionate and cherishes his children. These Christians believe that the attributes of God are just characteristics that God carries on his shoulders because they don't see the manifestation of these attributes in their personal life. The reason for that is that these Christians stand far away from God, without knowing that Christianity is a religion of individual relation with Jesus. These Christians choose to go by their will and desire that the Holy Spirit no longer moves them. They become so insensitive to the work of the Holy Spirit that only their brain directs their path. That's why Jesus says to the disciples:" **Whoever finds their life will lose it, and whoever loses their life for my sake will find it.**"

# Chapter 3

# A Troubling Dream

Dreaming is very complex concept. Dreams are a complex phenomenon that every man and woman experiences daily. Because of their complexity, I don't believe too much in dream interpretation. In Western civilization, little consideration is given to dreams. They are some psychological moments we all go through in our stage of slumber. According to psychologists, our state of slumber comprises three or four stages. Our dreams spring out in the third stage, leading to our stage of awakening. They have no importance and need no consideration. This concept needs to be genuine. Dreams are significant in the life of human beings. Every morning, when we wake up, we should examine thoroughly the dreams we have during our sleep time. Some dreams have a veil of deep meaning; sometimes it's the dreamer's spiritual state. Dreams with deep meaning have to be considered highly important. The story of Joseph in the Bible is a typical example that shows that not all dreams are vague experiences without meaning.

When he was a young boy, Joseph saw through dreams what he was going to be in adulthood. He saw through dreams how high he was going to become so that his father and brothers could live under his authority. Although his brothers didn't like the dreams, they pushed Joseph to accomplish those dreams.

We have four different sources to our dreams daily. The first source is our human spirit. Our own spirit gives us dreams all the time we go to sleep. These dreams originate from our senses and thinking. Things that we think about during the day can turn into dreams at night, and the TV shows we love watching every day can turn into dreams. Things that we visualize in our minds can become dreams in the night. Those kinds of dreams are senseless and meaningless. Most of the time, they are unorganized and lack cohesion. The second source of dreams is demonic. The goal of demonic dreams is to inflict fear and doubt on our inner person. Evil spirits use dreams to make us believe in lies. They authorize all lies and work hard to transmit them to humanity. Dreams of terror come from evil spirits. Dreams in which someone is chasing you down the road, and you are out of breath are demonic. Dreams in which a snake bites you on your leg indicate that the hedge of God around you are giving way due to your behavior. It means there is an opening in the protection of God around the dreamer. A Christian can grant access to evil spirits that can demolish the protection of God and infiltrate the life of the Christian. A Christian who is watching on TicTac a video posted by an evil spirit will receive a visitation of the demon at night.

The third source of dreams is purely satanic. Satanic dreams are dreams coming from witches and wizards. By nature, these dreams are very short, in which a Christian is in the company of some joyful people. When he wakes up in the morning, the Christian will realize that some of the people in the dream are dead without Christ. Sometimes, the Christian dreams of seeing himself in the cemetery with other people he doesn't recognize. After these dreams, the Christian will start feeling sick or complain about feeling something strange in his body. Doctors will perform analyses after analyses, but the results will state negative. The implication is that this Christian is under witchcraft attack. Someone in witchcraft intends to harm the Christian, and the witch has access to the Christian. Sometimes, the witch doesn't want to kill the Christian but wants to destroy the Christian financial life. A Christian has to wake up and fight back in prayer when he's having those dreams.

A schoolteacher told me that the day he received his salary from his job, the following day, his sickness started. He would go from doctor to doctor, from hospital to hospital. The day he spent his last dime on medication, the illness disappeared. This teacher would borrow money from friends and family members to make it to work until the end of the month. Following the day he received his pay salary; the sickness would resume.

The fourth source of dreams is the Holy Spirit. The characteristics of dreams coming from the Spirit of God are clear and vivid. They aim not to cause fear or manipulation. They always have a deep meaning that only the Holy Spirit can explain. The more the Christian doesn't understand the dream, the more the dream will repeat itself. The repetition of the dream continues until the Christian is disposed to want to know the meaning of the dream. Sometimes, the Spirit of God doesn't give the meaning of the dream when it's a mountain top for the Christian. The Holy Spirit refuses to explain when it's a stage where the Christian will be down the road. And the road is being confirmed, and there is no turning back or deviation from the plan of God. When the dream of God repeats itself, it means the place the Christian is going to is already in place, and nobody can change it. The heavens have decreed it, and no change can come from somewhere.

I had some dreams that I couldn't determine the source of. Were they from my spirit or the Spirit of God? I couldn't tell. According to my habit, before bed, I would read a portion of the Old Testament, and in the morning, I would read a portion of the New Testament. Sometimes, in my dreams, I would see myself mingling with biblical characters. The biblical passages I read before bed would become a reality in my sleep. One night, I dreamt that I was among the crowd of the Baal worshippers on Mont Carmel when the prophet Elijah was offering his sacrifice (**1 Kings 18:1-46**). I could see Baal adepts exhausted from yelling at Baal unsuccessfully all day. They sat on Mont Carmel, heads down on their shoulders, wearing red and black ribbons on their foreheads. They watched the prophet Elijah build an altar to offer his sacrifice to the God of Israel. Elijah was building the altar when I woke up from my sleep, around 4:15 in the morning. Another night, I dreamt I was in the middle of the eleven children of Jacob going to Egypt to buy grains (**Genesis 43:1-34**). We were in a minivan, and Ruben, the older son, was in the front seat next to the driver. I didn't know who the driver was, but I wasn't interfering in the conversation of the eleven brothers. There was an argument back and forth in the vehicle. Ruben would turn to his brothers in the back, pointing at Simeon. He would blame Simeon or another sibling. The argument continued until we reached the gate of Egypt, and I woke up.

Here is another dream where I could relive all the decisive moments of the children of Israel crossing the Red Sea (**Genesis 14:1-31**). The night the Israelites were leaving Egypt, the Lord God unleashed millions of angels flying over Egypt, creating an impetuous wind. Sometimes, these angels flew over the Red Sea, waiting for a signal to act. They received specific orders from God. The children of Israel looked lost when they reached the Red Sea shore, and the Egyptians believed they had wedged between land and sea. Informed about the geographical situation of the Israelites, Pharaoh chased after the children of Israel with about six hundred chariots. The Egyptian soldiers also camped by the seashore, separated from the Israelites by a column of fire.

Then, God told Moses to stretch the staff in his hand over the Red Sea. When Moses raised the staff, the angels flying over Egypt ranged into two rows and were attached to one another. With high speed and force, the angels hit the water's edge. The Red Sea split in two when the two lines of the angels separated, leaving a dry land between the two rows. A line of angels on the left and the right, the children of Israel started walking through the Red Sea. The children of Israel were walking through until they had a significant advance to the other side when the column of fire left the Egypt side to the Canaan side. At first, the Egyptian soldiers were hesitant to go through the Red Sea. But, at the command of Pharaoh, they went in chasing down the children of Israel. At this point, the first sun rays started to be visible. When the Israelites saw the Egyptian chariots crossing the Red Sea, they ran faster to the other side. But God had another plan in place.

Any chariots that ran faster to reach the last Israelite walking through the Red Sea would receive surprises from the angels blocking the water flow. When a chariot got too close to an Israelite, spontaneously, an angel from the left and from the right would stretch out their hands to snatch the wheels of the faster chariot. Before this scenario, many Egyptian chariots were breaking down in the middle of the Red Sea. The two riders of the broken-down chariots would get down to try to fix the chariots to catch at least one Israelite. The increasing number of broken-down chariots caused the Egyptian soldiers to realize that the Lord God was causing the breakdown. They all abandoned their chariots and started running back toward Egypt when Moses withdrew his staff over the Red Sea. There was a lift at that instance, and all the angels holding back the water took off. A mighty splash resulted when the two water columns smashed into one another. The Egyptian soldiers could not survive the blow, and they all drowned in the Red Sea. The collision was so severe that even the chariots broke into pieces and flowed on the water's surface. Although good swimmers, the Egyptian soldiers didn't have the chance to swim. There was chariot debris and inert human bodies flowing on the surface of the Red Sea. All the children of Israel could see the deliverance the Lord God had performed for them. Instantly, the Israelites boasted in praise and worship unto the God of Abraham, Isaac, and Jacob. Mary, the sister of Moses, started singing, and the rest of the women joined in. The whole assembly up roared, singing and dancing.

The sources of our dreams are numerous. Every Christian should consider the kind of dreams they are having. Some dreams have essential meanings that Christians shouldn't disregard. A Christian who has two nightmares every week should have the help of his spiritual mentor. The mentor or Pasteur will diagnose the origin of the nightmares and pray to close the door to any evil spirits.

# Chapter 4

# Jesus before Pilatus

When I read the gospels, I often try to understand Jesus' behaviors in different situations and circumstances. Many of his behaviors trouble my spirit. For example, Jesus is sleeping when the boat is rocking, and water enters the ship. The disciples fight to get the boat on the water and ensure the ship doesn't sink. They try everything possible in their power and knowledge. They are all exhausted when they turn to Jesus to state that they are perishing. Jesus stands up with his two hands in the air and speaks to the wind and the waves. And a perfect peace covers the sea. The disciples gaze into one another's eyes and ask themselves, who is this man, Jesus? Another is when Jesus stands before Pilatus in a trial before his crucifixion. Before Pilatus, Jesus decides not to answer Pilatus's questions. The accused refuses to answer every question Pilatus is throwing at Jesus. But Pilatus makes a statement that pushes Jesus to answer. Jesus reacts to Pilatus's statement, but why? It's in John 19:10-11.

**"Do you refuse to speak to me?" Pilate said. "Don't you realize I have power either to free you or to crucify you?"**

**11 Jesus answered, "You would have no power over me if the above did not give it to you. Therefore, the one who handed me over to you is guilty of a greater sin."**

People inflict a lot of evil things on Jesus prior to his death; he doesn't retaliate. Some people spit in his face, but he doesn't reply. The Roman soldiers mock him but doesn't react to the mockery. The Roman soldiers cover his face with a dirty rag, and they slap Jesus. Then, they ask him to guest, who slaps him. Jesus knows who slaps him but doesn't react to the mockery. The Roman soldiers whip him with a whip that is tearing his flesh, but he doesn't respond to the beating. The high priest and the religious leaders bring false accusations against him, but Jesus doesn't react to them, although he knows they are false accusations. The crowd chooses Barrabas, a thief and murderer, over Jesus. But Jesus doesn't respond to the crowd's choice, although he knows it's wrong. The Roman soldiers are nailing him to the cross. Jesus is going through an excruciating pain when the nails are going through his hands and feet, but he doesn't react to all of that. He says no word concerning all those mistreatments. But Jesus responds to Pilatus's statement: **"Don't you realize I have power either to free you or to crucify you?"**

If Jesus reacts to Pilatus's statement, there must be a hidden message behind Pilatus' words. I know there must be a mystery to unveil in Jesus's reaction. So, I start seeking the Lord to grasp the meaning behind Jesus' response. I search different prophecies concerning Jesus' death to find a clue. I turn to Esaiah 53:7:

**"He was oppressed and afflicted, yet he did not open his mouth; he was led like a lamb to the slaughter, and as a**

sheep, before its shearers are silent, so he did not open his mouth."

I searched the Old Testament for a clue to Jesus's behavior before Pilatus. Many prophecies describe him as a lamb going to slaughter and a sheep before its shearers. According to the descriptions in the prophecies, Jesus must be quiet and not open his mouth until death. But Pilatus's statement causes Jesus to open his mouth. The controversy causes me to start praying to the Spirit of God to reveal the meaning behind Pilatus's statement. There must be something I need to know in the confrontation between Jesus and Pilatus. It takes a little while for the answer to come. The answer I get wipes out many other questions I have been dealing with.

Many bad situations we see ourselves in sometimes come from God or are the will of God. Some circumstances are a perfect orchestration of the Father. Standing before Pilatus is an orchestration of God the Father. It doesn't result in the power of Pilatus; it's a perfect will of God. He is standing at Pilatus's judgment seat as a means for Jesus to get to the cross. Pilatus doesn't have power over Jesus, but he is an instrument God utilized for Jesus to get to where he is supposed to be. All human beings go through challenging situations that God coordinates for a purpose. In particular, Christians face challenges in their lives to prove their belonging to the kingdom of God. It's like a test all Christians have to undergo. It doesn't matter if the Christian is poor or rich, intelligent or unintelligent, humble or arrogant, shy or outspoken. God has a specific test for every category of Christians. Some fail miserably on their test, and others pass brilliantly their test. The tests help God to determine the state of mind of a person and the rational relation with other persons and God.

Nobody on planet Earth can fool God. Our test results look like a spectrum where we can fall into the far left, the far right, or in the middle. The area where we fall in the Spectrum will determine our next test. If a person passes his test, he will fall on the positive side of the Spectrum. If a person fails the test, he will fall on the negative side of the Spectrum. The spot where a person falls on the Spectrum determines the next test. These tests help God know people or Christians to reject or accept. In the rejection stage, we see King Saul in Samuel's book.

1 Samuel 13:11-12 **"What have you done?" asked Samuel.**

**Saul replied, "When I saw that the men were scattering and that you did not come at the set time, and that the Philistines were assembling at Mikmash, 12 I thought, 'Now the Philistines will come down against me at Gilgal, and I have not sought the Lord's favor.' So I felt compelled to offer the burnt offering."**

King Saul is in a great dilemma that God himself has orchestrated. The enemy army is marching against him, and the Vaillant and strong soldiers Saul counts on are in panic and running away from him. Samuel, who is supposed to come and offer the burnt offering before the battle, doesn't show. Samuel put together all he needs for the sacrifice at the appointed time, but God holds him down. God wants to know what is in the heart of this new king, Saul. Miserably, King Saul fails his test and takes the responsibility to offer the holocaust, although he is a Benjamite. Saul is not a Levite. His failure causes him the kingship. So, God rejects Saul as a king over Israel, and he starts looking for an ideal king. He finds David, son of Jesse, as king over Israel.

A friend of mine took me to an Assembly of God church in Florida. The service was excellent, and the praise and worship team were phenomenal in choosing the songs we performed. Before preaching God's word, a woman came to the podium to testify to God's goodness. The woman said her husband was on a business trip for a week. This was the first time he was away for that long. The couple had a son, who was about ten years old and a well-fed boy. While the father was away, the boy had a cardiac attack at night and couldn't breathe properly. The woman tried to resuscitate her son, but the boy wasn't responding. She panicked and didn't know what to do. The family doctor's office was closed, and the husband wasn't picking up his phone. So, she called an ambulance to come and take the boy to the hospital. The paramedical team arrived within less than ten minutes of the call initiative. They put the boy on a stretch and rolled it inside the ambulance. The mother wanted to ride with the son in the ambulance to the hospital. The paramedical crew declined the mother's proposal. She took her personal vehicle to follow the crew to the hospital. By the time they all got to the hospital, the illness symptoms had vanished, and the boy recovered. The lady was delighted and wanted to thank the Lord for her son's life.

Before the woman finished her testimony, the Holy Spirit told me, "That woman just failed her test."

It seemed that the woman was living her Christian life in the shadow of her husband. But God wanted to know what was exactly in her heart. He wanted to know who she would call on first when she was in trouble. God wanted to know who she trusted the most: her medical insurance, family doctor, or the hospital. God wants to know who we trust the most.

On the positive side of the Spectrum is Father Abraham. God tests Abraham to determine what kind of man he is. God asks Abraham to sacrifice his beloved son Isaac on a specific mountain, the mountain of Moriah.

**Genesis 22:11-13 But the angel of the Lord called out to him from heaven, "Abraham! Abraham!"**

**"Here I am," he replied.**

**12 "Do not lay a hand on the boy," he said. "Do not do anything to him. Now I know that you fear God because you have not withheld your son, your only son, from me."**

**13 Abraham looked up, and there in a thicket, he saw a ram[a] caught by its horns. He went over and took the ram and sacrificed it as a burnt offering instead of his son.**

God has tested Abraham, and he passed. God asks Abraham to sacrifice his son Isaac, and Abraham obeys the order God has given him. The passing of his test gives Abraham the attribute of a righteous man before God. When the angel of God calls Abraham from the heavens, he tells him not to harm the boy, Isaac. He also tells Abraham that a ram is attached to a tree for the sacrifice behind him. Abraham doesn't go into the bush looking for the ram destined for the sacrifice. But, when Abraham turns his head, he can see the ram in the bush. The ram isn't hidden, but it's just behind him. But why Abraham doesn't visualize the ram there?

1. Abraham is overwhelmed by the idea of losing his beloved son Isaac. God has already accommodated the way out of every test a Christian goes through. For every challenge a

Christian encounters, there is a provision for the situation. But many Christians don't realize that God is in control over the problem they are going through.

1 Corinthians 10:13 **No temptation has overtaken you except what mankind expects. And God is faithful; he will not let you be tempted beyond what you can bear. But when you are tempted, he will also provide a way out so that you can endure it.**

The promise in this verse doesn't apply to someone or a Christian living in sin. A Christian who impregnates a minor and is serving time in a state prison will not expect a way out from God. God desires the Christian to serve the correct time for the offense. A Christian should pay for his crime and not expect God to bail him out.

2. Abraham can't see the ram because it's not given to him to see. We have to understand that the invisible world determines the visible. What the heavens decide is what will occur. God doesn't give Abraham the opportunity to see the ram caught in the tree. In our lives, some things are given to us, and others aren't. It's the rule of nature. The twelve apostles of Jesus face the dilemma of knowing who Jesus is. It's not given to them until Jesus dies and rises from death before the veil is removed from their eyes. For, if they really know who Jesus is, they will fight to prevent the death of the Messiah. Were they knowing who Jesus was, the Roman soldiers would have to crucify them before Jesus would go on that cross.

Up to today, the Baptists I have come out of believe that speaking in tongues comes from evil spirits. They preach against all gifts of the Holy Spirit. I don't blame them because they don't grasp it. There are things that are given to a person and things that aren't given to the same person. As long as God doesn't remove the veil from their eyes, they will keep fighting against God.

2 Chronical 32:31

**But when the rulers of Babylon sent envoys to ask him about the miraculous sign that had occurred in the land, God left him to test him and to know everything that was in his heart.**

King Ezekiah loves God and devotes his life to His service. The scriptures affirm that he walks with the integrity of King David. He has done what is good in the eyes of the Lord. God gives him victory over all his enemies. God is before him in all his battles and overcomes all his adversaries. When Sennacherib, king of Assyria, rages war against Ezekiah, God takes over the fight and sends only one angel against the Assyrians. Then the angel of the Lord comes out and puts to death a hundred and eighty-five thousand men in the Assyrian camp. Despite the excellent relationship between King Ezekiah and the Lord God, Ezekiah goes through a test for God to see what is in his heart.

Now, the question is, why does God put his children through tests? The answer is more challenging than it may seem. The first answer is that we are in the selective stage of our lives. In this stage, God is selecting people who love him unconditionally. He is looking for people who love him from the bottom of their hearts, with their souls, minds, and power to be with him. He wants people who deserve his love to constitute his kingdom. The second answer is that God promises to ensure no sin enters his paradise. He goes beyond and above to make sure no sinner can slip or side through the gates of his kingdom. God tests Christians and non-Christians to ensure they can live with Him in his dwelling place. He is a holy God and can't deal with anything unholy.

1 Corinthians 6:9-10: **Do you not know wrongdoers will not inherit the kingdom of God? Do not be deceived: Neither the sexually immoral nor idolaters nor adulterers nor men who have sex with men nor thieves nor the greedy nor drunkards nor slanderers nor swindlers will inherit the kingdom of God.**

The third reason God puts his children to the test can be found in the authority He granted his children. God is very interested in what all of His children are capable of. He wants to know who can endure a tough time, a hanger, a tribulation, a beating, and much more. These are some criteria by which God offers his calling and authority to people. He wants to know if the person is fit for the job before He grants the person power and authority.

# Chapter 5

# Fierce is the fight, and the higher is the blessing

When I was a young boy in Togo, my mother told the story of two cousins living in Lome, the capital city. The two cousins were thieves. They didn't hold jobs and were professional thieves. They went into people's houses at night to rob them while they were asleep. The two men were very crafty in what they were doing. They were so reserved that no one knew they were thieves. Every day, they went out together to search for their targets to rob. They identified the nice and rich houses in different areas of the city. They looked for houses where they could find a lot of money and a good quantity of jewelry. They knew where to sell gold and diamonds to make money. Their wives knew what they were doing at night to bring money home. The wives wouldn't participate in their husbands' robbing plans. One day, a fight broke out between the two cousins. No one knew the origin of the battle since the two men were so close and wouldn't share the source of their success with anybody. One of the wives broke the fight and asked the men why they were fighting. It was through persevering and nagging that a wife got out of her husband the reason for the fight. It turned out that the two cousins disagreed on a particular house on the city's outskirts. One cousin thought the house must be a wealthy dwelling to rob. But the other cousin disagreed because he thought the house wasn't rich enough to waste time and effort. Since the two cousins decided to steal people's houses for a living, they promised one another not to go into poor people's houses. They wanted to steal people who had valuable possessions.

The devil does the same thing. It doesn't go to poor people's houses. Instead, it goes into wealthy people's homes to kill, steal, and kill. If the devil attacks hard or fights fiercely against a Christian, the Christian possesses a treasure in his life. The devil doesn't waste its time on just anybody but on people equipped with skills and abilities. Christians who have no specific calling suffer a little in the hands of demonic forces. But a Christian with an extraordinary calling suffers multiple blows from all directions.

1. The suffering of Hannah in the hands of Peninnah.

1 Samuel 1:6-8

**Because the Lord had closed Hannah's womb, her rival kept provoking her to irritate her. 7 This went on year after year. Whenever Hannah went up to the house of the Lord, her rival provoked her till she wept and would not eat. 8 Her husband Elkanah would ask, "Hannah, why are you weeping? Why don't you eat? Why are you downhearted? Don't I mean more to you than ten sons?**

Peninnah has sons and daughters, but the Lord God closes Hannah's womb. Peninnah takes advantage of Hannah's weakness to provoke her daily. She will find a little occasion to bring Annah down. As first wife, Peninnah enjoys being in control of Elkanah's household. I can imagine a typical scenario in Elkanah's household.

Hannah cooks a delicious soup for herself and her husband at her doorstep. Peninnah's children are playing football in the house. The children throw the ball to one another. By mistake, the ball hits Hannah's soup on the fire. Luckily, the soup doesn't spill on the ground, and Hannah quickly kicks the ball away and says to the kids:

- "Hey, children, be careful, don't throw the ball too hard. It's almost hit my soup on the stove," Hannah says.
- "We're sorry. We don't mean to hit your soup," the children reply.
- "Come and get your ball, children," Hannahs adds. By that time, Peninnah storms out of her room to face Hannah.
- "You're threatening my children? Do you know what a good woman goes through to give birth to a child?" Peninnah asks.
- "I'm not threatening any of these children," Hannah answers.
- "You barren women never know how to care for children," Peninnah adds while walking away.

Then Hannah goes into her room and cries to God to give her at least one child to delight her heart. In every little situation, Peninnah brings Hannah's barrenness to her face. Again and again, Hannah goes to her inner room and shares tears abundantly before God. The problem is that Hannah doesn't know God has a calling in her life. She doesn't realize that God Almighty has all His eyes on her. Hannah carries a gene that can make a great prophet. At that time, God was looking for a great prophet who could quickly receive the word of the Most-High God. God values Hannah so much that He wants to use her beautiful genes to create a mighty prophet before Him. That's the reason why God closes Hannah's womb. God doesn't want any of Peninnah's children. Hannah is the chosen one, but he lets herself be mistreated by the unwanted one. God wants Hannah to make a deal with Him and promise to give God her first child. So, God lets Hannah go through the abuse of Peninnah until she realizes what to do. God orchestrates the situation to get what He wants; Samuel is one of Israel's greatest prophets. God is working behind the scenes because He has never punished Peninnah for the abuse.

Hannah's situation occurs in the lives of many children of God. They go through challenging situations because God has instilled a great gift in them. Because of their talent, God closes some doors before them. These Christians don't know that about themselves, and they want to be like the other Christians. You're going through what you're going through because of your calling.

2. Why God didn't defend innocent Joseph in Potiphar's house?

Genesis 37:26-28

**Judah said to his brothers, "What will we gain if we kill our brother and cover up his blood? 27 let's sell him to the Ishmaelites and not lay our hands on him; after all, he is our brother, our flesh and blood." His brothers agreed.**

**28 So when the Midianite merchants came by, his brothers pulled Joseph out of the cistern and sold him for twenty shekels[a] of silver to the Ishmaelites, who took him to Egypt.**

Joseph suffered tremendously at the hands of his brother. He was humiliated and rejected by them. The brothers sold him to Ishmaelite traders, who took him to Egypt. Then, in Egypt, Joseph was sold to Potiphar, a great man in the Pharaoh's government. Because of Joseph, God blessed Potiphar's household. Everything flourished in the house. The livestock produced a significant number. The farm yielded a better result. Potiphar realized that all the blessings he was getting came through the hands of Joseph. Besides, Joseph's physical attraction was glowing. Potiphar's wife couldn't resist the charm of the Hebrew boy in the house.

At first, the woman tried to seduce Joseph but failed lamentably. Though away from his family and land, Joseph kept his relationship with God alive. He wasn't angry at God for what he was going through. She lied to her husband when Potiphar's wife realized she couldn't draw the boy into sin. She lied on Joseph that he attempted to rape her in broad daylight when the husband was at work. The lie caused Joseph to be imprisoned. Why didn't God defend innocent Joseph? Why didn't God speak to Potiphar at night, in a dream, that Joseph was innocent? God did for Abraham and Jacob in the past. God didn't defend Joseph because the prison was the means to Joseph's greatness. The prison was for his good days. It was the tunnel to Joseph's great days. God defended Jacob in the hands of Laban in Genesis 31: 24.

**Then God came to Laban the Aramean in a dream at night and said to him, "Be careful not to say anything to Jacob, either good or bad.**

When Jacob quietly left Laban's house with his wives and children, Laban became furious. He gathered his relatives, whom he armed to pursue Jacob. They chased after Jacob for seven days and caught up with him in the hill county of Gilead. God intervened to warn Laban about attacking Jacob and taking from him all his possessions. God did almost the same thing for Abraham in Genesis 20:6-7 when Abimelech took Sarah for a concubine.

**Then God told him in the dream, "Yes, I know you did this with a clear conscience, and so I have kept you from sinning against me. That is why I did not let you touch her. 7 Now return the man's wife, for he is a prophet and will pray for you, and you will live. But if you do not return her, you may be sure that you and all who belong to you will die."**

God didn't intervene in Joseph's case because it was for a glorious day in Joseph's life. When you're going through challenging situations as a God-fearing Christian, know it's for a great day. You must go through a deep valley to reach the mountain top. Most of the time, God shows his servants the mountaintop, leaving the details of the valley to Himself. If you know the details of your valley, you'll not be eager to get to your mountain top. You'll not to go to the mountaintop.

3. The tie-down colt and Jesus rides to Jerusalem.

**As they approached Jerusalem and came to Bethphage and Bethany at the Mount of Olives, Jesus sent two of his**

**disciples, 2 saying to them, "Go to the village ahead of you, and just as you enter it, you will find a colt tied there, which no one has ever ridden. Untie it and bring it here. 3 If anyone asks you, 'Why are you doing this?' say, 'The Lord needs it and will send it back here shortly.**

The colt was tied to a pole at the village's entrance. Since his birth, no one has ever taken him out to the town, rode in his back, or used him to do work. He has been posted at the entrance of the village since his birth. He chatted with all the colts and donkeys that went to the town daily. The other colts and donkeys would narrate new things they experienced out of the village every day. When the other colts and donkeys returned from the city in the evening, they would make fun of the tie-down colt.

- "You're still here? You've never gone out to see new things that happen?" They say.
- "I'm praying one day my Master will take me out", the tie-down colt replies.
- "Prayer will not do it for you", they will add.
- "What can I do, my friends?" The tie-down colt will say.
- "You can ask your Master to take a ride on your back to the town".
- "He doesn't want to take me out."
- "You can break your chain and leave the village at least once to see new things."
- "Now, I will get his attention so he can take me out to experience new things."
- "If you can break your chain, we'll find somebody to ride you to the city."

The tie-down colt doesn't know he has a calling in his life. He thinks he is just an ordinary colt like the other colts in the village. He despises his condition of being tied down to a pole all his life. Every day, his Master brings him food by the village entrance. The Master brings him water after he eats. He wants to behave like the other colts. The tie-down colt wants to go out and see what's happening in the city. He wants to see how different the city is from the village where he has lived all his life. He is tired of his life where there is no change or excitement. He wants to change his life condition to the image of the other colts and donkeys around him. He ignores that his condition is for a purpose. He doesn't realize that his condition is for a glorious day. He doesn't know he is a famous colt that many prophets have spoken about in the Old Testament. He doesn't know that he is the set-aside colt that will one day take the Master of the Universe, Jesus Christ, on a triumphal ride to Jerusalem. The tie-down cold doesn't know that no one should ride him before Jesus. If any man has ever sat on him, the Messiah wouldn't sit on him anymore. If any man has ever used him to work, Christ wouldn't sit on him anymore. The tie-down colt has a divine purpose that causes him to be tied down.

Many Christians do the same things today. They don't like their life condition and don't know why they are in such a situation. These Christians are on the phone daily, telling friends and family members about what isn't working. They complain to the wrong people and look for the wrong solutions. Instead of being quiet and seeking the Lord, they open their mouths to curse themselves or to speak blasphemies.

Your joblessness is because the position God wants to give you isn't vacant yet. Your celibacy is because your bride isn't ready yet. Your barrenness is because your first child has a calling to bring one of his elementary teachers to Christ. The repossession of your vehicle helps you avoid an accident the enemy has planned for you. The tardiness of your promotion is because God wants to get you the highest position in your company. People of God quit complaining and listen to the voice of the Holy Spirit.

The words of encouragement in this book are meant for born-again Christians who live their lives according to the word of God. I'm addressing the concerns of children of God who have devoted their lives to the gospel's cause and are going through tough times. I want them to know that God is aware of the challenges they're facing. Sometimes, He is the author behind your troubles, watching to see who you'll lean on or who you fear the most.

Many Christians that I encounter live half their lives in the world and half in the word of God. Today, they are in Christ, and tomorrow, they are in the world. It's so hard to determine which side they are on. They are look-warm Christians; they're not hot or cold. These Christians get into trouble that God hasn't intended for them. They bring hardship and tribulation they could avoid just by living in righteousness. I have seen Christians steal staff in the workplace. If a Christian goes to jail for stealing from an employer, it isn't considered a tribulation or test from God. It's the consequence of the Christian's misconduct. And God isn't the author of your jail time. You bring the trial and tribulation on yourself.

# About the Author

P hilip C Sossou was very fascinated with literature at an early age. He holds a master's in African Literature from the University of Lomé. In grad school, he led exciting research on African means of transmitting cultural values from one generation to another. In his early academic life, Philip was influenced by famous African authors like Chinua Achebe, Ngugi wa Thiongo, and Ayi Kwei Armah. Later in life, at El Camino College, he embraced well-known American writers: Helen Keller, Paul Anderson, and Henry James. Philip learned from them the art of creating images with words. He wrote a dynamic critique, "Daisy Miller" by Henry James, to give his students the desire to venture into Literature. As a schoolteacher, Philip Sossou lured many of his students to build their skills in writing essays and dissertations.

Printed in the United States
by Baker & Taylor Publisher Services